HOW TO GET FROM HERE TO THERE WITHOUT GOING ANYWHERE

A Simple Guide to Living a Happier Life

Carrie Rose

All rights reserved. © Carrie Rose 2013

Cover design © Aaron Phull

No part of this document may be reproduced, sold, stored in or introduced into a retrieval system, or transmitted, in any form or by any means (electronic, mechanical, photocopying, recording or otherwise), without the prior permission of the copyright owner.

Disclaimer: Although the author has made every effort to ensure that the information in this book was correct at press time, the author does not assume and hereby disclaims any liability to any party for any loss, damage, or disruption caused by errors or omissions, whether such errors or omissions result from negligence, accident, or any other cause.

This book is not intended as a substitute for the medical advice of physicians. The reader should regularly consult a physician in matters relating to his/her health and particularly with respect to any symptoms that may require diagnosis or medical attention.

First printing: 2013.
ISBN-13: 978-1494319540
ISBN-10: 1494319543

British Cataloguing Publication Data
A catalogue record of this book is available from
The British Library.

Also available on Kindle from Amazon

To my son - who I love to the moon and back

To my husband – who is the calm to my storm (Gmily, Gaily and Geily – he knows!)

To my clients - who teach me so much

WHAT THEY SAY ABOUT 'HOW TO GET FROM HERE TO THERE WITHOUT GOING ANYWHERE'

"Money can't buy you love but this happiness guide by Carrie Rose COULD actually make you happy. It's not about counting your blessings but discounting your curses. Why not start giving yourself an even break today? Carrie will show you how."
Phillip Hodson, Fellow of the British Association for Counselling and Psychotherapy

"This is a great addition to the self-help books around – easy to read, light-hearted but with depth and compassion. Carrie shows humility and expertise, humour and empathy in her writing. I particularly liked the exercises, which are very accessible but also powerful. I know I will be recommending this book to clients and using some of the exercises too."
Jackie O'Carroll, Flourish Coaching

Carrie's belief is that we all have what we need inside us right now to live a happy, successful and fulfilled life. We just need to know that it is inside, not outside us, and how to unwrap our own treasures. Carrie gently shows you how to do this and is living proof that it is possible.
Nick Williams, author of eight books including "The Work We Were Born To Do" and co-founder of www.inspired-entrepreneur.com

"Carrie explores so many areas of potential personal growth and with the clear, simple exercises at the end of each chapter, it is a really fascinating journey which leads one to a deeper understanding of how we 'tick' and how we can change our reality through changing our thinking and 'programming'. What is also refreshing is how she shares her own personal experiences, helping us to realise we're not alone in our struggles and issues! A thought-provoking book to inspire and coax us to be the best that we can be!"
Tanya De Leersnyder, Iyengar yoga teacher, aromatherapist and founder of Kalya products

"Inspirational, comforting and honest. A delight to read with many guiding, practical and helpful insights for everyone – no matter who they may be!"
Karen Ezard, Communication Skills trainer, consultant and mediator

"'How to get from here to there without going anywhere' is a lucid and delightful read. Based on Carrie Rose's distilled wisdom as a practitioner, the book identifies the range of blockages in our own personal growth, provides compelling and fun exercises to enable the reader to really engage with the material, and signposts a positive way forward."
Grahame Dixie, Advisor at The World Bank

"Carrie's book makes it amazingly easy to gain the awareness to identify the walls we set up that stop us from living the lives we want. Read the book, reflect, learn and MAKE THOSE CHANGES!"
Gunilla Thor-Finch

"Carrie's enthusiasm for helping people to create a better path in life shines through in her book, as does her gentle, nurturing approach. Also the exercises at the end of the chapters are really helpful to actually get thoughts and feelings on paper."
Anna Thomson, District Nurse

"This is a book we can all relate to that addresses in a sensitive way the feelings and experiences we all have. Using simple exercises, it is an easy to read practical guide to achieving a more fulfilling life in which Carrie delivers a very real message, using well chosen meaningful examples."
Sean Kelly, Business Growth Consultant and Coach

"Carrie Rose writes with great intimacy, warmth and clarity. She encourages you to stop chasing the future and to live in the present. This is how we create a better future. It's all about milking the sacred NOW!"
Robert Holden, author of Happiness NOW! and Holy Shift!

ACKNOWLEDGEMENTS

Perhaps it's only when we spend time with the express intention of being thankful that we realise just how many people we are thankful to, for so many reasons. That was certainly the experience for me in writing these acknowledgements.

So many people have supported, helped, encouraged and believed in me writing this book. To mention you all would be a book in itself. To name a few, my heartfelt thanks to:

My father, who cared. My mother, who loves with a big and generous heart. My step-father, who does so much for us all. My brother, who gives. My husband, who makes it all work. My son, who is my miracle. My stepson, who brings music into our lives.

Gunilla Thor-Finch, Karen Ezard, Kay McMahon, Grahame Dixie, Jackie O'Carroll, Tanya De Leersnyder, Phillip Hodson, Anna Thomson and Dorothy Cowen.

My marvellous mentor, Sean Kelly.

My caring coaches, Pam Lidford and Lisa Sorensen and to all at Canfield Coaching.

My magnificent media person, Laura Rettie.

My divine book designer, Aaron Phull

And finally special thanks to my brilliant book coach, Alison Thompson (The Proof Fairy), without whom this book would not have happened

CONTENTS

INTRODUCTION	11
CHAPTER 1 - WHERE DO WE BEGIN?	19
CHAPTER TWO - BELIEFS	25
CHAPTER THREE - FEAR	34
CHAPTER FOUR - THE MYTH OF NOT GOOD ENOUGH	44
CHAPTER FIVE - YOUR INNER CHILD	55
CHAPTER SIX - OUR MANY SELVES	68
CHAPTER SEVEN - HEAVEN AND HELL	85
CHAPTER EIGHT - EGO AND THE HIGHER SELF (otherwise entitled 'Get out of your own way')	95
CHAPTER NINE - YOUR COMFORT ZONE AND BEYOND	106
CHAPTER TEN - DECIDE WHAT YOU WANT AND DO IT	119
CHAPTER ELEVEN - LIVING RIGHT HERE, RIGHT NOW	131
CHAPTER TWELVE - SOME THINGS TO HELP YOU ON THE JOURNEY WITH NO DISTANCE	136
CONCLUSION	144
ABOUT THE AUTHOR	145
RECOMMENDED READING LIST	146

INTRODUCTION

"The truth is that the world wants you to succeed and be happy. The responsibility lies with you to open yourself to the possibility."
Ben Renshaw

What attracted you to this book? Did you like the idea of something 'simple'? Does the word 'happier' leap out at you? Or did you just fall for the witty and clever title?! Whatever your reason, I'm assuming that you're reading this book because somehow you want something more from life.

If so, read on because this is a book for anyone who would like to live a happier life but doesn't want to meditate on a mountaintop to achieve it. It's a down-to-earth guide for anyone who feels that there has to be a better way of living but is not really sure what that is.

I believe that most of us are searching in many different ways to find happiness – whether we know that's what we're doing or not. However, the search is needless because all we need for that seemingly elusive happiness is with us here and now – and always has been. To borrow author Mandy Coulbeck's book title, 'Happiness is an inside job'.

That's all very well, you may say. You get the general idea that no matter how many pairs of shoes you have in your wardrobe, or how powerful your car engine is, it isn't ultimately going to do it for you. Not in a way that has any ongoing, lasting, positive impact on you. But what *is* the answer then and how do you go about finding it?

In a practical and easy-to-follow way, this book presents a set of ideas and tools to show you, the reader, the wealth of abilities, resources and gifts you already possess to lead a happier, more fulfilling life. It looks at the ways we have skewed thinking, leading to misery and unhappiness, and presents solutions as to how we deal with those thoughts to create that happiness we're seeking. It is aimed not so much at the spiritual seeker but at anyone who's asked themselves the question "Will I ever be happy?" and seemed unable to find the answer.

So what is this happiness we're seeking? Perhaps before we go too much further it would be helpful for me to describe it from my perspective. It's a word we use a lot but it's difficult to define, isn't it? I think of it as having a sense of being at peace with ourselves; having self-acceptance (this is who I am and I'm happy to be that 'who'); an ability to enjoy ourselves in the world and enjoy what the world has to offer and an ability to have great relationships – with ourselves and others. But perhaps, more than anything, being happy is being fine with ourselves and our lives right here, right now. That's not to say that we don't want to achieve – have, be and do – more. But our starting point is one of peace and contentment in the present moment, not one of lack, frustration, beating-ourselves-up, despair…

Having said that, I'm worried, very worried, about us all. Perhaps not the best way to start a self-help book (if *I'm* worried, what hope is there for you, the reader?!) but it's the truth. I'm so aware that we – and by that I mean the human race – are increasingly looking for happiness

INTRODUCTION

in all the wrong places. These days, more than ever, we're constantly being encouraged to have more, be more, do more – and then we'll be happy. Or rather, that's the implication. Perhaps we've all become so caught up in this trap of acquiring, whether it be the latest iPad, more channels on our TV, a better job, bigger car. Our lives have become so fast-paced that there's no time to ask ourselves, "What exactly am I doing this for? What am I hoping to achieve by all this acquiring?" If the answer is 'happiness and fulfilment' then we've bought into a collective myth that anything 'out there' in the world is going to be the source of lasting happiness 'in here' – in our hearts, minds, spirits.

There seems to be a growing dissatisfaction with the world in general and ourselves in particular. We're seeking to find the answers in anything from material wealth or the partner-of-our-dreams to the latest guru. But those all-important answers don't lie anywhere 'out there'. As a client of mine recently observed, "I am my magic wand." In other words, that client (through exploring her own route to happiness with me) discovered that she already had the answers. She could create happiness for herself using her own inner awareness and resources.

It's my aim with this book to help you find *your* own personal 'magic wand' – an awareness of yourself and all the inner resources, qualities and general fabulousness that you possess. But to do this we need to do a little internal spring-cleaning – open some doors to your mind that might have been firmly shut (or that you didn't know you had) and dust out some others that have nothing but cobwebs behind them.

It frequently astounds me that the human race spends so much time, energy and money on exploring and discovering new horizons in the world around us (fascinating though they are) with comparatively little time and energy being spent on exploring and discovering our inner worlds – what makes us the way we are; how our thoughts and feelings are shaped; how our past influences our present. It seems to me that gaining a depth of understanding and mastery over our inner world is the essential starting point for everything else we want to achieve 'out there' in the world around us.

Time and time again, when I'm working with my clients (individuals, couples, groups) and witnessing their challenges and struggles, I feel so sad that we're not taught more in school about how we tick as humans. It would save so much misunderstanding, heartache and pain. Not all of it – because I think that everyone's lives has times of difficulty, challenge and, yes, pain. But so much is self-inflicted through lack of self-awareness, and through simply not knowing or understanding what it is that makes us think, feel, act, react, respond the way we do.

So I'm writing this book partly because of what I've come to understand through working with my clients during my years as a counsellor, life-coach and course leader but also because of my own life experiences, including my struggles and challenges and the ways I've learnt to make sense of them, work with them, and find greater happiness and well-being.

I think it is part of my life purpose to want to impart knowledge to

INTRODUCTION

others, to support, nurture and inspire people to live happier, more rewarding and fulfilling lives and my first awareness of this came at a very young age.

When I was a child I had a recurring film playing in my head that if only I could find a high enough mountain and scream loudly enough "STOP!" then all the wars and fighting in the world would end. I actually believed that I had the power in me to make that happen – if only I could find that mountain.

In a way, I still have that same conviction today. Beneath my layers of 'human-ness'– my self-doubt, fear, uncertainty – there's a part of me that believes I have the power and ability to change the world. It's from this child-like part of me (sprinkled with some more adult understanding and observations) that I write this book. I actually believe that we all have that power and ability in us. It just lies dormant, waiting to be discovered but instead, for the most part, gets buried deeper and deeper. As to why that happens and what to do about it, well, you'll just have to read the book to find out!

Fast-forward from childhood to me at seventeen. A seemingly happy, fashion-led, boy-mad schoolgirl. Much like your average schoolgirl then. Except I remember thinking very clearly "There has to be more to life than this?" and then somehow I managed to bury the question for another ten years. Easily done. Some people manage it for a lifetime. It is, after all, a tricky and challenging question to answer. But then a friend nagged, cajoled and twisted my arm to take part in a personal development seminar called 'Insight' and my path was set. It was sometimes rocky and occasionally it petered out, but it was a path that couldn't be 'got off' (no matter how hard I tried at times!).

I realised during that seminar that, apart from the occasional existential question about the meaning of life (ten years earlier), I hadn't paid much attention to my inner world at all. I barely recognised that it even existed, let alone realised just how much impact and control it had over how I saw and experienced my life. That seminar opened up a whole new world for me – the world of my inner self. All the thoughts, feelings, beliefs, ideas I had about who I was and how the world around me functioned were suddenly highlighted. So I went from not even knowing that I had all of this inside me to beginning to recognise just how much all this 'inner stuff' shaped my sense of self and the world as I saw it.

Since then, I've taken part in countless personal development seminars, training courses and spiritual retreats. My bookshelf groans with vast quantities of self-help books. And they've all had value and helped to shape my understanding of myself and others and the way we create our experience of the world.

Since training professionally as a counsellor and life-coach, I've been fortunate to be able to take that understanding to a deeper level, through my work with my clients. One of the most wonderful, inspiring and moving aspects of my job is to be able to see in my clients that everything they're looking for is already there. It is a huge privilege to be able to sit with someone, feeling the pain and confusion they're experiencing and yet seeing that they already have their answers. They're already everything that they're looking for. Or, to put it another way, they have everything they need to create everything they want. So if I have one wish for you as a result of reading this book, it's for you to know that you already have everything you need to create a happy life. You don't need to go anywhere, do anything (except some internal 'furniture shifting') or be anyone other than who you already are.

I want to say upfront that this book probably doesn't contain anything that, at some level, you don't already know. However, you've either temporarily forgotten it or didn't know that you knew it in the first place. My hope and intention is that the book will remind you of an inner truth, that as you read it you'll be saying, "Yes, I get that. Yes, that's me. Yes, that makes sense. Yes, that really is true." Many years ago I remember reading my first ever self-help book, 'Living In The Light' by Shakti Gawain, and it was as if she was ringing some inner bell of truth at the core of my being that I'd ignored until then. I felt that I'd known this truth all along but didn't know I'd known it. I hope this book will have that effect on you – it's a book to remind you of what you already know about yourself and your ability to be happy. You'd just forgotten it, that's all.

It's also a book to increase your awareness of how you live and the choices you make on a day-to-day basis. Without awareness we're puppets, with the strings being pulled by our sub-conscious minds. I want to help you to be your own puppet master. Awareness is a master key to achieving everything we want to have, be and do in life.

Some chapters may speak to you more than others but I encourage you to persist. Take what works for you and discard the rest. Much like shopping for new clothes, you only need to browse briefly through the rails that aren't your thing, stopping to pay more attention to the ones that are just what you need. However, again with clothes in mind, it might be worthwhile trying an idea on for size even if you think it isn't right for you. The mind can play funny tricks if it wants you to avoid something.

Before you continue on to Chapter One, a word about the exercises in this book. Each chapter concludes with an exercise relating to the chapter topic. I ask you to put aside any notions of homework or something you *should* do. Instead I suggest that the exercises are done in a spirit of playfulness and curiosity and exploring with interest this being called 'you'.

Reading is a great way to engage your mind, activate your inner knowing and expand your awareness about yourself. Doing the exercises is about making this information even more personal to you and getting every last juicy bit from the chapters. It's an opportunity to understand more about who you are and how to live your life in the best possible way. And who doesn't want to do that?!

CHAPTER 1 - WHERE DO WE BEGIN?

"It's time to start living the life you imagined."
Henry James

Often when a client comes to see me for the first time, they will sit down and say to me: "I don't know where to begin." Barely a moment's pause and then it all starts to come tumbling out – everything that the client is thinking and feeling at that moment, all their challenges and fears, concerns and anxieties. At times the client will be in crisis, feeling that they just can't cope any more. As I sit and listen with empathy and compassion for their pain and confusion, I begin to sense two people. The first is the person they think they are – everything that currently overwhelms them and shapes their thoughts and feelings. The second is the person they are beneath the layers of protection, beliefs, fears and self-doubt.

As my client continues to talk about their life, I'm also, in a sense, two people. The first is caring and supportive of them in their pain and beginning to piece together the jigsaw of how they came to be where they are. The second 'me' simply holds the truth about them – that they have everything they need right here, right now in order to live the life they want. That 'me' knows that no matter how self-critical they are or how much their lives seem to be in a mess, everything they need to sort it all out is sitting there in front of me.

These days I often say to my clients early on: "*You* think this crisis is the worst thing that has ever happened to you. *I* think it's an opportunity and that something is calling you to make much-needed changes, not necessarily to your external life but to the way you think and feel about yourself." I'm surprised by how many people, even through their pain, actually agree with me. I sometimes go as far as to say (taking my courage in both hands) that I think their crisis is a gift. It's very moving to see how often some wiser, more knowing part of my client responds with "It's true." Even if they look at me in bewilderment at the time, they will often acknowledge later that their crisis has indeed been a much-needed gift.

So where are you in your life at the moment? Where shall we begin with you? Are you simply feeling that life isn't as good as it could be? Are you feeling that you 'should' be happy but somehow you aren't? (A client said to me recently, "Everyone tells me that I have everything I need to make me happy – a loving partner, good job, lovely home, but…" As if, once we complete the checklist of things required to make us happy, we automatically will be.) Are you full of anxiety and fear, self-criticism and doubt? Or are you, like many of my clients when they first come, going through a crisis?

Wherever you are, I want to start by saying to you it's OK. There is a way back. There is a way to achieve contentment, inner peace and, yes, that elusive happiness. And it's surprisingly simple.

But, as with my clients, you need to start with where you are and take a long, honest look at your life as you see it. The reason that you are where you are is largely because of all the things you think and feel about yourself, the beliefs you have about yourself and your life.

CHAPTER ONE – WHERE DO WE BEGIN?

Starting to feel uncomfortable? Is this beginning to feel a bit challenging? Well, let me say to you this bit *can* be challenging but I promise it will be worth it!

At this point, I want to say that some of you might be going through difficult and painful events. Perhaps someone you love has died or you're getting divorced or are dealing with illness. It's understandable to be feeling loss, sadness, fear, loneliness but, even so, the way you deal with and come through these situations will be greatly influenced by your approach to your life. Perhaps it is at these times, more than any other, that reviewing what you're telling yourself and looking at the 'story' you've created about your life can be immensely valuable.

For example, if you're experiencing a bitter divorce, how much are you blaming the other person? The 'it's all their fault' approach helps us to feel better about ourselves in the short-term. If it's all their fault then it can't possibly be your fault and therefore you're still a good person whereas they're the bad guy. However reassuring this approach might be, it doesn't allow us to ask ourselves important questions such as "How did I contribute towards this? What was my part in the breakdown of this relationship?" This isn't about apportioning blame (a particularly fruitless pastime. You might as well count grey hairs for all the benefit you'll get). What these questions do is enable us to start accepting responsibility for our life, for how we create and shape it according to the decisions we make.

"But he was a bully," you might say. So what was it in you that was attracted to a bully? What part of you allowed yourself to stay and put up with his bullying? What part of you wanted to play the victim? This level of honesty with ourselves isn't about beating ourselves up about our decisions but acknowledging and accepting that we've had our own part to play in whatever we've created in our lives.

What I'm saying is that, in order to free ourselves from the feeling that life happens to us and that our happiness is dependent on some external source, we need to take complete responsibility for our choices and our actions. What if we create, promote or allow everything that happens in our lives? That can be quite a bitter pill to swallow when we first consider the question. But if we are to be the author and instigator of our own happiness (and honestly, if it's not down to us, then who else would it be down to?) then taking this approach, alongside feeling like quite a responsibility, is also the source of our emotional freedom and well-being. The bad news is it's all up to us. The good news is it's all up to us. How exciting and empowering is it that we are potentially the source of our own happiness and wellbeing? How liberating is it that it isn't dependent on anything or anyone else?

Start to understand that how you see yourself isn't the truth of who you are but a series of beliefs and assumptions you've made about yourself as a result of your life experiences. The 'you' you believe yourself to be is, at least in part, based on a story you've been telling yourself, a story that you've been writing, chapter by chapter, as you've gone through life. Obviously our life experiences do have an impact on us and help to 'shape' us, at times in a positive way when we

CHAPTER ONE – WHERE DO WE BEGIN?

learn and grow through the things we've been through. But all too often, from a very early age, the stories that we create about ourselves aren't helpful. They hold us back, limit us, make us scared and convince us to play small in the world.

If we were able to take a stroll as a visitor through the inner sanctums of our minds I think we might be horrified by the 'litter' we find there. All the rubbish we've taken on board about ourselves and our lives would be clogging up the space, stopping the flow of peace, joy, love, well-being that is naturally meant to flow through our minds. If we are to realise the potential that we always have had and always will have for inner peace, fulfilment and happiness, then we have to recognise this debris for what it is and brush it aside to reach the golden nugget that lies quietly awaiting us when we take the time (and find the courage) to pick up the broom.

So I ask you, as you continue through this book, to imagine standing back from this 'self' you've created and observing him/her with curiosity, interest and, most definitely, compassion. As the saying goes, "If we could have done better, we would have." Make a commitment right now to be willing to understand yourself in a different light, one that will bear fruit as you go through the chapters. Here's to you, the true you, and finding that golden nugget.

Exercise

Imagine you are sitting with me (or someone you feel able and willing to confide in fully, whether real or imagined). What would you tell me about your life? How do you see yourself? What are your concerns and fears, doubts and worries? Are you feeling depressed, anxious, stuck? Or are you sad, lonely, scared? Is it that you have a longing, a yearning, to get more from life and maybe being OK just isn't good enough. It can be helpful to say this out loud so you can really 'hear' yourself. Perhaps record what you're saying so you can listen carefully to what you've been telling yourself. Or, alternatively, write it all down. Don't censor anything; just write about yourself and your life as you see and feel it. You might feel a sense of relief simply from having put into words some of those unnamed feelings. You might re-read what you've written and think, "Is my life really such a mess?" Or you might think, "Well, it's all alright but I'm sure it could be so much better." Whatever your response, you've taken the first important step, which is to honestly acknowledge where you are (or where you think you are) in your life right here, right now.

CHAPTER TWO - BELIEFS

"It's not who you are that holds you back.
It's who you think you're not."
Denis Waitley

Now that we're daring to take a look inside that dark, cavernous, scary place called our mind, we begin to realise that much of what it contains are beliefs rather than facts. As we travel through life, it can become increasingly difficult to separate the two. Fact: the earth is round. Fact: I am shy. Well, is that a fact or is it something you've come to believe about yourself?

Perhaps more than anything else that is within our control, developing a deep awareness of the beliefs we hold and the way they shape our reality plays a crucial part in leading us down the (inner) path to happiness.

We start off in life as our brand new shiny selves with all our gifts, qualities and unique offerings for the world firmly in place. If we were to exist in an environment of complete love, support, acceptance and encouragement from day one to adulthood, it would be easy to express ourselves fully, to have a strong sense of self-worth and to live in the way that we were meant to. That innate self, the self we were born to be, would remain intact and untarnished.

Unfortunately for us, no one has that sort of perfect environment to grow up in. It simply doesn't exist. So our thoughts about ourselves become shaped by our experiences. By the time we've reached adulthood, most of us have been through challenging emotional situations and as a result we've taken on board all sorts of beliefs about ourselves. If we've been frequently put down then we might begin to believe that we're stupid. If we've been over-protected, we might come to believe that life isn't safe. If we've been constantly pushed to succeed, we might believe we have to forever strive to do better.

Whatever the belief we've absorbed, the end result is the same. We begin to think those beliefs are who we are or how the world is. But they're just stories we've been told and, because we didn't know any better, we believed them. So we gradually become less ourselves (the self that we came into this world to be) and start acquiring layer upon layer of false beliefs which we wear like an invisible cloak. Eventually we end up operating on automatic pilot, not questioning how we've come to see ourselves and the world around us. We hold on to those beliefs as if they were facts about us rather than fiction that we've convinced ourselves is true.

However, it isn't all dire. Remember that golden nugget? It's not that it got lost along the way. We didn't leave it behind in childhood. We simply buried it. Or perhaps it would be fairer to say it got buried, because as children we have no idea that we're doing this. We're simply reacting and responding as best we can to the world around us.

The beliefs we hold keep us imprisoned in our inner dens of unhappiness. Beliefs that, if we could find the key to the door and shove them out of it, would leave us a whole lot better off emotionally and well on the way to happiness and well-being.

It's great to see the penny start to drop with my clients when they begin to realise just how much of the way they see themselves and the world is not set in stone. It's not a reality but, like a house of cards, built of many layers which have no solid foundation. "So I don't have to believe I'm stupid just because my teacher told me I was?" "I don't have to think I'm useless because my mother said so?" "I don't have to believe that the world is a scary place because that's what my father taught me?" Once my clients get the hang of standing back from their lives and observing what they believe, they rapidly start to discard beliefs that don't work for them.

However, that then brings up another question: "If I'm not who I believed myself to be then who am I?"

When people ask themselves "Who am I?" I think the more useful question is "Who am I when I'm being me?" In other words, we all have times of experiencing being ourselves – when we feel natural, in the flow, relaxed and at ease. It's the times when we believe that we *should* be a certain way or ought to act in a particular manner that we lose touch with our sense of self. I think it's ironic (as is much about the human psyche) that we often behave the way we think we should or ought to in order to be accepted and fit in. And yet, it's when we allow ourselves to be our natural, authentic selves that we shine the most and are appreciated and valued more by others.

So all you need to be is YOU! That unique, essential you doesn't have anyone it can measure itself against in terms of success and failure because only you know how to be you. Being you isn't about being perfect or trying to get it all right (you never will). It's about embracing every quirk and flaw, acknowledging and celebrating the richly complex and multi-layered being that you are. 'You' is your gift to the world. Don't allow something that isn't and never has been true to hold you back from fully being yourself – and living a fuller, richer, more rewarding life as a result.

Most of us have acquired and accumulated many limiting beliefs by the time we reach adulthood (and often well before that). I thought I'd give you some examples:

LIMITING BELIEF EXAMPLES

I'm not clever/attractive/rich/young enough

Women don't do that sort of thing

I can't do anything right

It's not OK to focus on my own needs

I should hide what I'm really feeling

I'll never be wealthy

Everyone else can do this but me

What I think isn't important

I have to be bright and bubbly all the time

I haven't got what it takes to succeed

CHAPTER TWO – BELIEFS

Everyone else knows more than me

Recognise any? Once we become aware that this flotsam and jetsam is floating around in our minds, we can begin to get our nets out, catch it and chuck it away – the further the better. It all has its origin at some time and some place in the past, whether from parents, siblings, teachers, friends – it really doesn't matter. All that matters is that we recognise just how and when these beliefs limit us and decide to make a better, wiser choice about how we want to see ourselves and our lives.

I think that what we believe about ourselves and our lives is significantly responsible for our present circumstances – good and bad. Either we live a life dictated by the beliefs we hold or we decide to take charge of those beliefs and only keep those that are to our benefit.

An example of acquiring a limiting belief in my own life… When I was about twelve, a relative said to me, "You're just like your father, you're always late." And guess what I came to believe?! To this day, I can fall into the 'I'm always late' trap but if I do choose to be on time and not buy into that belief then of course I can be on time.

A friend, Martyn, recently described to me how he went on a singing course, not reading the small print and realising that by the end of the course the participants would be writing and performing their own songs and recording them. Had he known, he said, he would never have signed up for the course because he believed that he wasn't particularly musical. He could barely read music let alone write it, couldn't play an instrument and was definitely, in his mind, not a song-writer.

By the end of the course he'd written about ten songs and recorded his favourite. Martyn described the experience as if there had been a door in his brain marked 'song writing' which was locked, bolted, nailed closed, cobwebbed, and clearly labelled never to be opened. Yet somehow, with support and encouragement, he had found the ability to open it. Martyn found himself in a situation (by accident rather than design) which brought him up against a powerful limiting belief. He's now asking himself: "If I can write songs, what else am I believing I can't do which actually I can?"

What a great question. It brings us back to "Who am I?" in the most exciting, expansive way. How about looking at that question from the perspective of "Who could I be if I didn't hold myself back through beliefs that limit me? Who could I be if I only take on board beliefs about myself that are positive and helpful?"

Put another way, I love this question: "Who am I pretending not to be?" All those limiting beliefs we take on board lead us to pretend to be something other than us. But if we remove those thoughts from our minds then the pretence falls away and we can truly be us. Magnificent wonderful us.

So if we're no longer going to pollute our minds with limiting beliefs then obviously the thing to have is self-belief.

In the words of Napoleon Hill, author of 'Think and Grow Rich':

CHAPTER TWO – BELIEFS

"You can be anything you want to be, if only you believe it with sufficient conviction and act in accordance with your faith; for whatever the mind can conceive and believe, the mind can achieve."

If those limiting beliefs were acquired through a thought taking hold and a groove being dug in our subconscious with that thought embedded in it, then we can do the same with positive beliefs. What would we rather believe about ourselves? What messages of encouragement and support do you want to give yourself, to begin to lay down a whole new set of grooves in your mind? It's like over-writing an old CD and recording a new CD on top of it. It might need playing a good few times before you can really hear it but isn't that worth it when the end result is you living a happier, more rewarding life?

Some might say that people have to be born with self-belief. I would disagree. Self-belief is instilled into the lucky few from birth but the majority of us have to choose to have it and adopt an attitude-of-mind that leads us in that direction. Whatever our background, the past is the past and it's up to us now to take charge of what we believe, the thoughts we hold and the way we want to shape our lives.

So catch yourself in any moment when you're wavering or holding yourself back from doing something you know you'd really like to do – if only you had the self-belief. Ask yourself "What's the truth here? Am I really no good at public speaking or is that just a belief I have?" "Am I really not creative or is that just something I was once told?" Sometimes, gaining greater self-belief is about not allowing ourselves to be restricted by unhelpful thoughts we have running riot in our minds. At others it's about choosing to believe something better about ourselves. It's about changing the "I'm not someone who...." to "I AM someone who…"

A word here about confidence, something closely linked to self-belief. I frequently hear my clients say things like "I would do X or Y if only I had the confidence." As understandable as this statement is, it makes it sound as though confidence is something we do or do not have. Some lucky few have it. The rest of us do not. Well that's not how I see it. I think that this elusive confidence is something we acquire by doing the very thing that we feel lacking in confidence about. Don't hang around waiting for confidence to somehow magically arrive one day but take your fear by the hand (more about fear later) and step bravely towards whatever it is that you want to do. It's by the doing, the taking action, that we increase our sense of self-confidence. We find courage, we take a step, we feel proud of what we've achieved – despite not feeling confident enough to do it. And guess what? We somehow do feel more confident in ourselves and our abilities as a result.

Life is definitely not a waiting game. If we want to experience greater happiness, success, fulfilment, we need to take a leap of faith in the direction we want to go, whilst working on our self-belief and self-confidence, knowing that both will grow as we move forward. As Jack Canfield says in his excellent book 'The Success Principles' "Don't waste your life believing you can't."

Exercise

Think of a time that you achieved success doing something despite feeling that you didn't have the self-belief or confidence. Write about that situation. What was it that you did? How was it successful for you? How did you feel when you achieved success?

Now write down a list of the positive beliefs and qualities that you brought into play to achieve this success. Somehow, despite not feeling confident enough, you were able to motivate yourself to take action anyway. How did you do that?

Use the positive beliefs and qualities that you listed as a resource to move forward and re-create that success in different areas of your life. If you were able to uncover those beliefs and qualities once, they're still there to use whenever you need to. This isn't about you fooling yourself, using psychological tricks to convince you of something that isn't true. Quite the opposite. It's an exercise to remind you of what IS true about you, what's been hidden beneath the stories you've been telling yourself. If I told you there was a pile of diamonds hidden behind the curtains in your living room that are yours to claim but don't go near them, you'd think I was mad. It's much the same with self-belief. All you ever wanted is waiting 'behind the curtains'. You just need to choose to pull them back and claim your diamonds. Stunning shiny multi-faceted diamonds. Stunning shiny multi-faceted you!

CHAPTER THREE - FEAR

"Fear stands between you and your ability to go anywhere you like, do anything you want and meet anyone you please. To help you stay safe, fear motivates you to hide your essential nature by thwarting your ability to express yourself truthfully."

Rhonda Britten, author of Fearless Living

OK, this is a biggie, this thing called fear. I think most of us are aware that we're fearful of something or other but do you truly realise just how much fear might be holding you back in your life? I believe that our fears, both the ones we know about but perhaps more importantly our deeper, hidden fears play such a large part in keeping us stuck, hidden, small – and generally not very happy and fulfilled at all!

First of all it would be useful to take a look at what fear actually is. We frequently talk about being afraid of this or fearful of that (or if we don't admit it out loud, we certainly feel it). I've found an acronym that I came across years ago very useful in explaining fear. It's this:

F – Fantasy

E – Expectation

A – Appearing

R – Real

So that's mostly what fear is. We start off by imagining some future event – going for a job interview; being honest with a loved one; going

CHAPTER THREE – FEAR

on a first date; speaking in public. Then we let our imagination take hold and begin to create a negative fantasy about how that event might unfold. The more we think about this future situation, the more scary and difficult we make it. Most of us have a highly developed ability to create the worst-case horror story scenarios in our minds. We then get to the stage where we've shaped and evolved the horror story to such a degree that it feels real. This is where we really come unstuck because the feelings of fear, anxiety, terror, embarrassment, rejection start to flood into our minds almost as if we were experiencing that situation here and now. Whereas the reality is that we made it all up. However, by this time we're feeling so dreadful that the last thing we want to do is the thing we've been thinking about. We've convinced ourselves out of taking any action. Or, if we *do* take action, we're terrified. Isn't that a ridiculous thing to do to ourselves! We scare ourselves silly with some made up story, believe our own story and then let it stop us from taking any risks, living life to the full and growing into the amazing people we were meant to be.

Very often our fears take the form of something that might happen. Do you recognise any of these pesky little thoughts in your internal world?

I might fail

I might look stupid

They might not like me

I might not be good enough

> They might judge me
>
> I might succeed

(A strange one, this, but we are often as scared of success and what that might bring as we are of failure. Will we live up to people's expectations? How will our family and friends treat us? How will our lives change?)

> They might laugh at me
>
> I might end up broke
>
> I might not like it
>
> I might be scared
>
> I might feel ashamed

Once again, in making these statements to ourselves, we start to create the very feelings that we're guarding against (feelings of being judged, ashamed, laughed at…..) and then convince ourselves that it would be a Very Bad Idea to undertake whatever it is we'd been thinking of. In fact we can scare ourselves out of the idea of doing anything that feels remotely uncomfortable.

This fear business was also instilled in us from a very early age. As children, we frequently had adults around us saying things like "Be careful or you'll get hurt" or "Don't do that, you might fall." Of course all children have to learn that putting their hand on the oven or jumping off a ten foot wall isn't a good idea but unfortunately it's very difficult (if not impossible) to instil a sense of safety without instilling a sense of fear. So we develop inner gremlins that were planted in childhood but are long since past their sell-by date. Those gremlins are there to remind us to be scared so we don't take risks, get hurt or often do anything very much out of our usual (safe) routine. The problem with this is that we don't end up doing anything very much. We start to live a life full of 'if onlys' and 'it's alright for them' and 'I wish I could but...', not realising that we've boxed ourselves into a tight, narrow little world through our own imagined fears. Whereas if as adults we risk 'falling off the wall', it can lead to opportunity, discovery, growth and, at the very least, useful lessons for the future.

The other thing about fear is that it's very good at expanding itself. We think about doing something then allow a fearful thought to creep in and so dismiss whatever it was we were about to do. The next time we think about doing the same thing, we've already accumulated a level of fear which we add to, layer by layer, the more we think about whatever it is that we want to do. Without too much effort we have transformed our fear into sheer terror – and thus completely ruled out ever doing the thing that's terrifying us.

We can also allow ourselves to be swayed by other people's fears, which they then project on to us. Have you ever had someone say to you: "I wouldn't do that if I were you," and then feel yourself deflate and mentally toss your great idea in the bin? That person is often responding to you out of their own fear rather than genuinely putting themselves in your place. They are literally saying "If I thought about doing that, I'd feel scared." Without necessarily realising it, they're imposing their own fears on you.

So what's the answer?

Firstly, it's important to recognise and be honest about the ways we allow our fears to dictate to us, hold us back and force us to live unfulfilled, uninspiring, risk-averse lives. No more saying "That's just me." That's who you've believed yourself to be whilst you've been ruled by fear. But if you're reading this book there's a pretty good chance that you want more than that. You no longer want this thing called fear to shape your life. I believe that we all have so much unfulfilled potential lying just below the surface of our beings (humming away under our skin saying "Let me out!") and one of the best ways of unleashing this is to deal with our fears.

Secondly, we need to have a different perspective on fear. I'm not about to say that we need to banish fear from our lives. It's natural and part of our genetic make-up. Somehow, we've come to believe that fear is to be avoided at all costs. One whiff of fear and we run in the opposite direction.

We can spend our lives waiting to feel less fearful. Do you recognise "I would do X only I'm feeling scared at the moment"? The implication being that at some unspecified point in the future we'll no longer feel scared. Well, the bad news is that that unspecified fear-free moment just doesn't exist. Sorry! The good news is that we don't have to wait until then. Instead I believe that we need to walk in the direction of our wants, desires and dreams hand-in-hand with our fear.

CHAPTER THREE – FEAR

Imagine taking a small child to school for the first time. (You might be one of those lucky parents whose child couldn't wait to go to school but, if so, let's pretend you had a child who was feeling a bit anxious, nervous and scared.) You wouldn't say to that child, "Oh well darling, if you're feeling scared perhaps you'd better not do it." You'd take them gently by the hand and lovingly coax them in the direction of school, perhaps letting them know that they'll be fine once they're there and probably have a lovely day. You'd be motivated by knowing that school will be good for them, will help them to learn and grow and that they'll probably come skipping out at the end of school saying they've had a fun day. Well, it's just the same process for us adults (who still have that inner child in us, by the way, who continues to play a huge part in our lives – see Chapter Five). If we do find the courage to take our fear by the hand and take steps in the direction we're fearful of, we mostly find that the outcome is rewarding and well worth the effort.

Or sometimes we say to ourselves or others, "I would do X only I'm feeling too scared." My question would be: "What does *'too* scared' mean? What are you telling yourself when you make that statement?" All it means is that the part of you that wants to stay safe has created just high enough levels of fear to convince you that taking action is definitely Not A Good Idea.

Far from seeing fear as a no-go zone, to be avoided at all costs, I think that often the thing we're feeling the most fearful of is the direction we need to go in. Stepping towards our fears is part of what we need to do to live a rewarding and enjoyable life where we're fulfilling our potential. The thought that seems so frightening is actually coming from the part of us that's calling us to grow.

I recognise this well in my own life. Several years ago the therapy centre where I worked was being sold and I asked if I could buy all the chairs, knowing that 'some day' I would like to work with groups as well as individuals and couples. Well, those chairs stayed in my attic for several years, a symbol of the work I would do 'one day'. (Do you recognise this 'some day' and 'one day' syndrome?) It was only through having a session with my own coach when I was feeling stuck career-wise that I recognised the 'one day' needed to be 'today' and that I was quite simply scared.

So I found the courage to take action (a huge key) and went about creating a course and attracting participants to do it. (Notice that I used the word 'attracting' because once I'd decided to move beyond my fear – or at least to take it by the hand – participants for the course started showing up.)

All was going well until the week before the course. I had all the course material, I had course participants, and I certainly had the chairs. However, what I also had was a serious dose of fearful thinking. "Who am I to do this? What if it's rubbish and no one likes it? I don't even know if I'll be able to stand up and talk in front of everyone. Why did I even bother to decide to do this? I'm feeling dreadful."

But fortunately, even in my wobbliest moments, I knew that this was just the part of me that wanted me to stay safe (not get rejected, look stupid, feel worthless). It was putting up a damn good argument for chucking it all in and calling off the course. I also knew there was another part of me that still really wanted to do this, even though at the time it was buried under mountains of fear. This part knew it was part of my growth and learning, a huge opportunity to express more of 'me' in the world and give more of what I came here to do.

So I stumbled my way through the week and by the time the day of the course came, I was surprisingly calm. It was almost as though my protection mechanism i.e. fear creator knew that it had lost the fight. Yes, when it came time to present my course, I felt those butterflies in the stomach but nothing I couldn't handle. The evening went extremely well. The participants were engaged, inspired and definitely wanted to come back for the next instalment. And me? Well, by the end of the session I felt that I'd expanded internally. I felt somehow a bigger better version of myself as I'd allowed a part of me that had wanted a voice for so long to come out of the shadows. As I went to bed that night my final thought was "I'm more than my fear" and that's true for each and every one of us.

There is another aspect of fear that I want to mention in this chapter. I call this 'the external voice of fear'. This isn't something that begins as an internal whisper but as a loud and intrusive collective scream from the voice of the media. 'House prices crash' it shouts. 'Job market collapsing' it heralds gleefully. 'Country in the depths of recession' it crows. For some reason I can't quite fathom, bad news sells a whole lot better than good news. But make no mistake, this stuff is poisonous. Don't read it. "But it's reality," you may say. Yes, at one level, but we contribute to creating that reality. We read the headlines, feel scared, act scared and then live scared lives. We play our part in generating that fear by buying into it and helping to create more of it. We start to worry about our jobs, buy less, feel fearful about the future and become part of the problem rather than the solution. It becomes a self-fulfilling prophecy.

So I want you to recognise that no matter how 'bad' it seems out there, you have a choice. Do you want to see the world through fear-filled eyes or with a positive, uplifted vision for your own life and the world as a whole? There are people in the world who still thrive in difficult times. Choose for one of those people to be you.

Exercise

This one is simple – not necessarily easy, but simple. Write a list of everything you feel fearful about, especially those fears that are stopping you from moving forward in life and living it to the full. Go on, be brave, write them down. The first step in dealing with our fears is being honest about them.

For example, right now I know that the next step in my career is to do tele-seminars but I'm scared. If I can admit this, then I can start to do something about it. When I fool myself (except I don't really) into thinking 'I don't want to do tele-seminars' rather than admitting the truth then there's nowhere to go with that. I've created a full-stop in my mind by side-stepping the truth.

So tell the truth to yourself. (No one else is going to read this list unless you want them to!) What are you afraid of? Making that call; applying for that job; leaving that job; telling your husband/wife/partner something you're not happy about; being honest with a friend; doing a parachute jump… For most of us, it's a pretty long list.

Now choose the items on the list that are holding you back the most. (Clue: it's probably the ones that you're preoccupied with, where your inner voice is chattering "Well maybe I could" and then "But no I can't".) Write a second list describing how you'd feel if you did the things you were scared of. "If I ran a tele-seminar, I'd feel proud that I'd overcome another fear and made my desire to help others more important than my limiting beliefs." If you made that call, how would you feel? How might that move you forward in your life? If you were honest with your friend, how relieved might you be? Obviously we can't control the responses of others but we can acknowledge our own courage and ability to take a step, despite our fears.

Finally write a third list, again choosing the fears that you think are most holding you back. This list begins 'Despite my fears I'm going to…' and list the actions you're going to take. Tip: go back to the exercise in the chapter on 'Beliefs' and use some of those qualities and abilities you uncovered to support yourself in taking the steps.

CHAPTER FOUR - THE MYTH OF NOT GOOD ENOUGH

"Wanting to be someone else is a waste of the person you are."

Kurt Cobain

OK, so hands up if you've ever felt not good enough. Welcome to the human race.

Time and time again, in my work with clients, they will hit a 'reality' (reality in quotes because that's the way it feels to them but actually it's anything but reality) about themselves and I can see them crumble before my eyes. "I feel that I'm not good enough," they confess, perhaps never having expressed this thought out loud before. It's painful for them to acknowledge, both to me and to themselves, and I see the look of shame and embarrassment in their faces.

Then we explore this idea. "Not good enough for whom?" I ask. They don't know. "What makes you think you're not good enough?" I ask. Again, they can't answer. "Who are you measuring yourself against?" I ask. Here they might possibly say, "Anyone who I judge to be better than me," but again, more commonly, they will reply, "I don't know."

You see, when we start to examine this feeling, my clients begin to see that it's just a belief that they've acquired somewhere along the way and then, because they didn't know any better, have accepted without question. Sure, once we believe we're not good enough, we'll go on to gather all sorts of 'evidence' to prove it. "He got promotion whereas I didn't." "She's found a loving partner and I haven't." "He's wealthy

CHAPTER FOUR – THE MYTH OF NOT GOOD ENOUGH

and successful whereas I'm not." All these things can easily be used to convince ourselves of this insidious belief. And the more evidence we gather, the more we believe it.

Let's look at this particularly nasty form of lurking gremlin more closely. Do you think anyone is born 'not good enough'? Would you look into the eyes of a tiny baby and say "Aaahhh how sweet, but not good enough I'm afraid"? This 'not good enough' thing isn't something we were born with. We acquired it along the way just as you would an unwelcome friend who lurks around and eventually gets to hang out with you because you've become resigned to them.

It may be that you had parents who were critical and demanded a lot of you. It may be that you had siblings who were academically more gifted than you or better at sports or – anything that you could judge yourself against and come out seemingly lacking. It may be that your best friend at school was beautiful, brilliant and brainy. For whatever reason, somewhere along the line you either a) were given the message that what you did wasn't good enough, or b) you decided to compare yourself to someone else and come off worst.

Here it's so important to highlight and differentiate between two different levels of 'not good enough'. The first – feeling that something we've done isn't good enough – is debilitating and draining in itself. We frequently criticise and beat ourselves up for not having lived up to our own expectations (which mostly starts from not having lived up to someone else's expectations). It can become hard to embark on anything new because that nagging fear of 'it won't be good enough' is lurking in the shadows. However, the second level of 'not good enough' is deeply, deeply damaging and destructive. At this level, we have taken on board the belief that not only is what we do not good enough but who we fundamentally are as human beings is someone who is 'not good enough'.

I think there's another shadowy culprit lurking about propagating this idea and that's the world we've collectively created. Increasingly it's becoming a world that encourages us to compare ourselves to others – whether physically, mentally, emotionally, financially, even spiritually – and come off lacking. Of course this is largely a financially motivated directive. If you don't feel as good as X then throw some money at the problem to look more beautiful; feel more successful; have a better body. Have you ever done any of that and did it ultimately make the difference you were searching for? We both know the answer to that one.

In fact, following that path can make things worse than ever. Recognise any of this thinking? "Hell, I've spent hours in the gym, have a designer wardrobe and drive the car of my dreams but it still didn't do the trick. I still feel lousy – and now more lousy than ever because I've spent so much money trying to feel better about myself – and it didn't work."

As you read this, can you see the basic and fundamental flaw in this thinking? Well, it's all based on the idea that who you should be is something other than who you are. Whether imposed by others or self-inflicted, it's an equally ridiculous, damaging, life-draining and generally rubbish way to think. And it has to stop!

I was well aware before I started writing this book that I could suffer from a severe case of the Not Good Enoughs. After all, who was I to write a book about happiness when so many others (the great and the good) had trodden the same path before me? I could easily have fallen into the Pit of Comparison (a particularly nasty pit writhing with snakes that like to wrap themselves around you and squeeze out every last ounce of self-belief if they get half the chance). But then I stopped to laugh at God's joke. Of course I had to face up to these feelings if I was going to write a book about them. How could I be authentic if I wasn't able to say "I know how it feels. I've dealt with this too"? How could I write a book that was of any value if I hadn't had to move through and beyond everything that I'm writing about in order to share anything helpful or insightful with you?

To deal with this feeling of not being good enough I had to do some self-questioning. Was it true that I had helped many hundreds of clients to have happier lives? Yes. Was it true that that had happened because I was being me with them? Yes. Therefore was it true that I had something to offer that was unique and of value because it came from me? Yes, actually it was.

So it became very clear that if I was ever to write this book, I had to walk my talk and not let comparisons with my self-help heroes stop me from offering what is uniquely my take on this business called living our lives. It became clear to me that if I did that I was not only selling myself short but potentially denying others the possibility of a happier life. I'm not saying this in any grandiose way. I'm simply acknowledging that I have something to offer that has been helpful to others and could be helpful to you.

And of course, the same is true for you. (You've probably got by now that in sharing about my own life, I'm trying to say "If it's true for me then it's true for you because I'm no different from anyone else.") You have talents, qualities, abilities and gifts a-plenty which are all you need to live a successful and fulfilling life – if you'd only let yourself be you.

My client, Phillipa, grew to understand this when she came to see me because she was unhappy in her high-powered corporate job but didn't know what to do about it. She felt trapped by the need to earn a certain salary whilst feeling that she was slowly losing the will to live. (Not literally, thank goodness, but definitely in terms of her enthusiasm for and interest in her job.)

We started looking at what else she might do and began to explore her hobbies, interests and passions. It soon became pretty clear that cooking was her huge passion. When she spoke about food and cooking, her whole being lit up (a pretty strong clue that this was something to check out further!). We began to explore the option of setting up her own catering company but then she did some research and discovered that there were several other catering companies in her area. "Why should I set up," she asked, "when there are other great companies with excellent reputations already doing what I want to do?" She then began to feel that they would all be better than her too. After all, they had experience and clients. She had neither. All she'd done was cater for friends' events when they'd asked her to. She was sinking into a major pit of not good enough. Something had to be done – and fast!

So I suggested that she check out with her friends why they'd asked her to cater for their various dinner parties and events. They came back with answers like "No one makes a tiramisu quite like you," "Because you do it with such a quirky sense of fun and style," and "Because we love how passionate you are about the food you make." Hearing this feedback, Phillipa was encouraged to dip a toe in the water, printed her business cards, created a website and within weeks had her first client. She's now up and running full-time and having a ball (hard work though it is).

Phillipa observes: "I had to believe that I could be a success at running a catering company because I was doing it my way. I have my own unique take on how to run my business. My food will look and taste just that bit different from everyone else's, simply because I made it." She adds, "Dealing with the not good enough stuff has not only allowed me to create a whole new career but it's helped me to believe that what I have to offer, who I am, is absolutely good enough." Phillipa also learnt a good lesson in understanding that 'people buy people'. And what a great example of not comparing yourself to others; just learn from them.

So hopefully my and Phillipa's experience is helping you to see that not feeling good enough is a major waste of all that you are and all that you could be. But the Big Question, of course, is how do you actually stop feeling not good enough?

The first step is to simply understand that this is a belief you acquired. It – the belief – isn't you. I repeat. It is not who you are. It's a story that you've told yourself (or been told), adding further chapters of 'not good enough' (often including 'really not good enough', 'you're just the pits' and 'self-loathing') as the years have gone by. And after a while it becomes difficult to tell fact from fiction. For example, sometimes I ask myself whether the lost city of Atlantis is fact or fiction. I've heard about it so often that I really don't know if it's just a story or reality. It's much the same with our 'not good enough' thoughts. The more we think the thought, the more our subconscious soaks it in and eventually decides it must be true because it's heard it so many times.

So what if, instead, you were to adopt a more healthy belief about yourself. I am good enough. Because essentially, fundamentally, you are good enough to be you. And you is all you need to be. You see, this is so ironic because if, instead of all those years of niggling 'not good enough' feelings, you'd concentrated on being the best 'you' you can be, those 'not good enough' feelings would have dropped away anyway.

If I were to sit with you now and ask you to talk about the qualities, abilities and talents that you have, eventually you would be able to draw up a list. It's true that initially when clients come to see me they often say "I don't know what I have to offer the world." But after a

CHAPTER FOUR – THE MYTH OF NOT GOOD ENOUGH

little questioning, exploring, challenging and supporting, everyone will start to uncover some of the characteristics that make them essentially and uniquely them. The more they talk about these qualities, the more I can see them 'come alive'. Some spark has been (re)ignited. A memory, a reminder, a glimpse of who they really are – and it feels good.

In all my years of working as a counsellor and life-coach, working with individuals, couples and groups, there's one thing I know for certain. Everyone has something valuable, worthwhile and uniquely good enough about them. Part of the joy and the challenge of my job is that I can see that from the start. But it's not enough for me to tell my clients. They simply don't/won't believe me. They have to discover it for themselves. My role is to remind them of who they really are, to hold a mirror to them and say, "See, this is really you. You've been living in the hall of mirrors where all reflections are distorted. Here, have this nice, shiny, clean mirror that offers you a true reflection of yourself."

And the joy, oh the joy, when someone comes to a session and says to me, "I've got it!" They might then tell me about situations during the previous week where they've caught themselves thinking any of the multitude of variations of 'not good enough' and decided not to do that any more. They've decided instead to choose 'good enough to be me'. It's evident in their faces, I can see it in their body language, I can feel it in their energy – they've come alive, come back to themselves. They've changed their whole perception of themselves and approach to life (yes, it can happen in a week!), simply by no longer allowing themselves to believe the lie.

As with everything else in this book, it is ultimately up to you. What do you want to choose? To continue to not feel good enough, hold back, play small, live a life that at some level you know is less than you could be living? Or do you want to face the Not Good Enough monster head on and watch it shrink to a tiny speck, recognising that the only reason it was ever a monster was because you made it so? (I'm saying 'shrink' rather than 'disappear' because I think that most of us have the feeling resurface from time to time. The challenge then is to recognise what's going on as quickly as possible and make a wiser choice.)

You know there's a bigger, better, bolder life inside you. Dare to believe that you're good enough to live it.

Exercise

You know by now that I like to keep exercises simple. I see them as an opportunity to take everything I've been talking about in the chapter and apply it directly to you in a way that will actively help you to have a happier life.

So for this exercise I'd like you to write a list headed: 'If I felt good enough I would……..' Then complete the sentence with any thoughts that come to mind.

For example:

If I felt good enough I would….

CHAPTER FOUR – THE MYTH OF NOT GOOD ENOUGH

…..wear more outrageous clothes

…..ask for the promotion I want

…..trust that my friends like me for who I am

…..take a spa break

…..ask out the guy down the road

…..join a running club

…..spend my days being content with myself

Please don't hold yourself back. Allow yourself to really go for it. After all, you're only writing words on a piece of paper.

Now cross out the first heading ('If I felt good enough I would…') and write a second heading in its place: 'I *am* good enough to……' Then say each sentence out loud.

I am good enough to….

…..wear more outrageous clothes

…..ask for the promotion I want

…..trust that my friends like me for who I am

…..take a spa break

…..ask out the guy down the road

…..join a running club

…..spend my days being content with myself

You may feel initially that you don't believe what you're saying. That's understandable. You've been telling yourself the opposite for a long time. But keep repeating the sentences out loud and notice the times when you get a glimmer of "You know what, maybe I am good enough to….." That's a good sign. Notice too how much better you feel telling yourself these things than believing the first list. Bring as much energy and belief as you can to the statements. Say it like you mean it – even if you don't at first. The more you repeat your sentences, the more you'll start to realise that you'd far rather be saying and believing them than having your initial thoughts. Keep hold of the fact that what you believe about yourself is your choice. Why not believe the best?

CHAPTER FIVE - YOUR INNER CHILD

"A grown-up is a child with layers on."
Woody Harrelson

In all my years of working as a counsellor, one of the realisations that has had the greatest impact on my clients (and me) is that they have an inner child. No matter how 'grown-up' they consider themselves to be (and, if the truth be known, most adults don't consider themselves to be very grown-up at all. More on that later in the chapter.), there is always a child-like part of them too which can play a huge role in their daily lives. Once we come to understand a) that we have an inner child b) what this child is all about and c) how to live happily ever after with him/her, then we can gain greater mastery over our lives.

So what *is* this inner child all about? We generally think of our journey through life as a linear process. First we're born, become toddlers, infants, teenagers, adults and then we head towards old age and death. However, we neglect to understand that so much of our experience and the way we came to see the world as a child travels with us – almost as though we have our own child-like version of ourselves permanently tucked away inside us. The reality is that 'growing up' (linear) is more about 'growing out' (extending outwards).

We have at the heart of us that essence of us (the golden nugget), our essential nature with which we were born. Surrounding that, the first circle is made up of our childhood experiences which begin to shape our beliefs and approach to life. Then, in ever-increasing circles is the 'us' that we grow into – or believe ourselves to be – as we get older and go through further life experiences. So we may have expanded out through many life circles by the time we reach adulthood. But the first circle, created during our childhood, is the one that has been there the longest and often has the most powerful effect on us – mostly without us realising it.

At this point it's important to say that we're not looking to blame our parents (or anyone else) for anything negative we experienced during our childhood. Blame is a pointless waste of time and energy. The purpose of looking at our earlier life and the inner child who grew out of that life is to gain understanding and awareness.

As children we're sponges, soaking up everything that goes on around us, everything that is said to us and absorbing our experiences as we toddle through life. Because we are in an intense learning phase for our first few years and because we don't know any better, we accept all that we see and hear. We don't realise that what we're experiencing is just our family's/school's/friends' take on life – and so we internalise it all as though it were the truth about how life is. This becomes our blueprint, our guidebook for how life is as we continue on our way.

OK, you say, I can accept this idea but why does it have such a great impact on my life today? Why are you making such a big deal of it?

Two reasons:

1. We see the world largely through the lens of our childhood.

2. We often react to the world from our child-like place and, of course, so do others.

So let's look at these statements further…

Have you ever experienced inexplicable tears and felt 'very small'? That's your inner child. Have you ever given way to a foot-stamping, irrational type of anger (or at least felt it welling up inside you and struggled to control it)? That's your inner child too. Have you ever felt what you might have judged as inappropriately giggly, perhaps in a business meeting? Guess what, that's also your inner child.

Let me give you an example from my own life. I was going out with a girlfriend for coffee and then she casually mentioned, "Oh by the way, you don't mind if my friend comes along, do you?" Of course the 'adult' response would be "No, of course not." But I noticed a small shiver of trepidation and a real reluctance to say yes. Not because I disliked this other woman but because my inner child has an innate fear of being part of a group of three. And why would that be? When I was about twelve, I was very friendly with two girls at school, Carolyn and Alice. Carolyn was the golden girl, pretty, popular and clever (don't you just hate her already?) and Alice and I would vie for her attention and friendship. There was no end to the dirty tricks we would each play to win Carolyn's friendship (planting fake notes in Alice's desk – yes, I finally confess to it – and much more).

That three-way friendship was very painful for me and has left me with a deep dislike of being in a group with two others. However – and here's the better news – I understand what the feeling is about, I know where it came from, and I can now bring in my adult self to manage it rather than it (the fearful feeling) ruling me.

When I'm working with clients, if they start using phrases such as "It's not fair," "I just wanted to hit him," "I suddenly felt very small and tearful," or "Why do I find her so scary?" I know their inner child is present. It's not just about the words they use, I can hear it in their voice, see it in their body language and feel it in their energy. They just feel very young. I often ask them at that point "How old do you feel right now?" Frequently they will come up with an immediate answer. They just know. And mostly I do too. "Six," I'll think and "Six," they'll say. Everything about them at that point is six years old.

I then sometimes take them into an inner child exercise where they sit in one chair and imagine their inner child sitting in a chair opposite them. I ask my client to describe their inner child. What does he/she look like? What are they wearing? How are they feeling? Once my clients have got over the rather bizarre experience of talking to an invisible child sitting in a chair (and this usually takes a matter of seconds), it's extraordinary to witness how quickly they become engaged with the process. They can see this little person so clearly, describe their outfit in vivid detail, often adding comments like "She's swinging her legs on the chair right now" or "He's got a big bruise on one knee". This small being is very real and present to both me and the client at that moment.

I'll then encourage a dialogue between the 'adult self' (the client) and their inner child with the adult asking the child what's going on in

CHAPTER FIVE – YOUR INNER CHILD

their lives ("My mum's just shouted at me again and I'm hiding under the table.") and how they're feeling ("I'm feeling scared, bewildered, I don't know what I did to make her so cross.") and we continue to explore what that child is thinking and feeling. This is often the first time the 'child' has had the opportunity to express those thoughts and feelings and it can be an extremely moving, free-ing experience for my client.

Here's an example:

My client, Jenny, often reports feeling fearful and overwhelmed. When we explore this further she doesn't really know what she's fearful of. Her fears aren't anything she can name. And there's nothing specific to be overwhelmed by either. She actually copes pretty well with her life. When she does feel like this, she gets angry with herself, believing that she should pull herself together and stop being so stupid.

So in one session, when she's talking about these feelings, I ask her:

Me: Jenny, how old are you feeling right now?

Jenny: About five.

Me: And what happened to you when you were five?

Jenny: (suddenly tearful) I was sent to boarding school.

Me: Jenny, would you be willing to try an experiment to look at this a bit further?

Jenny: (a bit doubtful) OK.

Me: I just want you to know that we can stop this at any time if you feel too uncomfortable. OK? (Jenny nods) So I want you to imagine that little five year old Jenny is sitting in the chair opposite you. Can you describe her to me? What does she look like?

Jenny: She's got blond hair tied in plaits with a red ribbon and she's wearing a blue gingham dress. She's got white knee socks but one of them has fallen down and she's sucking her thumb.

Me: (to Big Jenny – BJ) What would you like to say to Little Jenny?

BJ: You look very small and very scared.

Me: Anything else?

BJ: You look like you need a cuddle.

Me: (to BJ) Please would you go and sit in Little Jenny's (LJ) seat.

So Big Jenny does so.

Me: (to LJ) Little Jenny, you've heard what Big Jenny has said to you. What would you like to say in reply?

LJ: I *do* need a cuddle. But I don't have anyone to give me one. I don't know why I'm at this school. No one has told me except that I've got to go. I really liked my nursery but now there are so many big children here and I haven't got any friends and the school is so big that I keep on getting lost. I want to go and hide under my bed and never come out.

Me: Have you told Mummy and Daddy how you're feeling?

LJ: They just say I've got to be a big brave girl and get on with it but I don't know how to and just wish I could go home. I'm scared. (She starts to cry)

Me: (gently) Would you like to hear what Big Jenny has to say?

LJ: Yes please.

So I ask Jenny to go and sit in the adult seat.

Me: Big Jenny, anything you'd like to say to Little Jenny?

BJ: I feel so sad and sorry for you and I'd like to give you that huge cuddle.

Adult Jenny then imagines her five year old self coming onto her knee for a great big reassuring cuddle – the cuddle she would have liked all those years ago.

After this exercise, Jenny tells me that she's never been able to express those feelings before because in her family you just had to get on with it and she thought it was wrong or weak of her to feel the way she did. Now, as an adult, she has huge compassion for the child she was. She also tells me that she can now understand exactly where her feelings of fear and overwhelm come from as she felt them so strongly when she was sitting in the five year old Jenny's chair.

Once we start to recognise that some of our more inexplicable, difficult-to-control feelings are actually those of our very-much-still-present inner child, we can begin to handle them just as a loving parent would with their frightened/angry/sad child. We begin to feel compassion for ourselves rather than frustration, self-awareness rather than bewilderment. Just as we would if we were actually parenting this child, we can lovingly take charge rather than being bowled over by feelings that we don't understand.

And, as I mentioned earlier, if this is true for us – that we have an inner child – then of course it's true for other people. This is so helpful in our relationships with others, whether at home or at work. Because guess what? Our inner child comes to work with us too. Haven't you sometimes felt that a colleague is behaving childishly? Well, in a sense, that's true. Their inner child will be acting out in some way or another if they haven't learnt to recognise, understand and work with it.

One common aspect of inner child that frequently comes out in the workplace is the bully. Have you ever had the distinct feeling of being bullied at work? The likelihood is that you were. Of course, bullying can be found at home, in friendships, between siblings and spouses too. Wherever you're experiencing it, the root cause is the same. Either that person learnt from a young age that the only way they could get their needs met/get attention/feel important was to be a bully. Or that person was bullied themselves at school and they're getting their own back (You hear the childish language? "I'm getting my own back on you.") on the bully all those years later by becoming a bully themselves. Sad but often true.

The way to handle that is to recognise that somewhere inside this seemingly dominant, demanding person is a small insecure child and

CHAPTER FIVE – YOUR INNER CHILD

that their behaviour is only masking those feelings. Stand up to them, as you would a bully in the playground. Show them that you're not going to be intimidated by their threatening behaviour. Notice too if this brings out any inner child feelings in you, like anxiety or fear. Then you need to 'parent' your inner child too, letting it know that it's safe and you can look after it.

If we are to lead happy and fulfilling lives, recognising and understanding when our inner child is running the show is essential. Then we can look after him/her with empathy, compassion and a good dollop of parental protection, letting them know that it's all OK because Mummy/Daddy is here to look after them – Mummy/Daddy now being the adult you acting as their loving parent. That really is what they need. We may not be able to see our inner child but they truly are alive and present – sometimes making themselves heard and felt more than at others – just like any child.

There is another aspect to our inner child which is equally, if not more, important. And I'm not telling you what it is! (Sorry, my inner child just came out to play!) OK, I will tell you. It's that our inner child is also a source of our joy, playfulness, creativity, enthusiasm, spontaneity, aliveness and ability to live in the moment. That's good news, isn't it! The more we stop telling ourselves that we have to be this supposed sensible adult and behave responsibly as an adult would, the more we recognise that all adults have this child-like part to them (and it's OK) and the more we can give our inner child the opportunity to shine.

If you want to know who you really are, how you were meant to live and express yourself in the world, go back to a time in your childhood when you were your most joyful, expressive, alive 'you'. Where were you? What were you doing? What were you wearing? How did you feel?

Don't worry if no memory comes to mind. For some people, childhood memories are difficult to retrieve. Perhaps you were treated in an adult way from such an early age that it's difficult for you to imagine truly being a child. Or perhaps your childlike-ness was quashed by parents who told you exactly how you should be and what you should do all the time. (I'm writing this feeling so sorry for those children, whilst recognising it's a tough job being a parent. You're never going to get it all right.)

However, I'm also aware that there are some adults who suffered through horrendous situations and experiences when they were small. Whilst my heart goes out to you, I want you to know that you can still get in touch with the child you were meant to be. That child was – and is – an innate, intrinsic part of you. Whatever the reason for lack of memory, the past is the past and you can still reconnect with your inner child.

If you've long had that feeling that you've lost yourself somewhere along the way, you're right. You did. You lost touch with the uniqueness, the gifts, the energy and enthusiasm, the creativity and in-the-moment-ness that your inner child has to offer. So much more of what you're looking for in life is available to you if you can allow

CHAPTER FIVE – YOUR INNER CHILD

yourself to live the way your inner child wants you to. I'm talking about all the good stuff that they have to offer, not the tears and tantrums.

Writing this chapter has really helped me to integrate another part of my inner child. As I was out walking one morning, thinking about what I wanted to write, I had a vivid image of me dancing under the stars to a live band on a hot summer's night in Majorca. I was six years old and dancing with all my heart, body and soul. So much so that everyone else cleared off the dance floor to allow me to fully express myself and (I fondly believe) because they were enjoying watching me. (It might have been because I was flinging myself about so much but I'll stick with my version of the story!)

I suddenly had a powerful realisation that that six year old was and is me – not just an intellectual realisation but one that I felt with every fibre of my being. She was expressing 'me' to the full, bringing to life all the parts of me that I had pushed into the background, ignored and locked away. When I acknowledged her and decided to let her be herself more fully in my life, I could almost feel her relief. She doesn't need to stay in the background any more and, as a result, I feel more powerful, more expressive, more me. If I hold the vision of her as my guide then if I'm feeling as alive as she did that night, I know I'm heading in the right direction.

So I really encourage you to do this work. It will make such a difference to you once you realise you have an inner child. Then you can learn to understand and befriend him/her rather than feeling that you have some inexplicable force lying dormant inside you that can erupt at any minute. Once you begin to acknowledge and have a relationship with your inner child, then you can start to bring more of their gifts into your life – their sense of humour, creativity, determination, self-belief, enthusiasm. Whatever it is that your inner child wants to express.

You will feel so much better for it – a sort of coming home to yourself. And there's another bonus. Whatever it is that you're meant to be doing in the world, you'll be able to do it so much more effectively with your inner child on board. However you're meant to contribute and share your gifts, they will have so much more impact on the world when you do so hand-in-hand with your inner child.

And one super-dooper final bonus. Life becomes much more enjoyable too. Because of course what do children like to do? Play, have fun, laugh, not take themselves too seriously (or seriously at all).

Q: Where did the king keep his armies?

A: Up his sleevies.

Exercise:

Please get out (or buy) the crayons for this one. And a big sheet of paper.

Remember a time from your childhood when you were expressing yourself as fully as possible, being every ounce of that incredible little you, and allow an image to appear.

CHAPTER FIVE – YOUR INNER CHILD

If you had a difficult childhood, imagine what you would have been like if life had dealt you a better hand. How *would* you have been if you were fully expressing yourself as a child, being your brightest, shiniest self? Imagine yourself independent of your life circumstances, perhaps taking yourself somewhere special (a beach, the zoo, a funfair – in your imagination, but why not do it for real too?) so that you can truly thrive. Give this child your full permission to really show up,

Now take your crayons and draw that little you and whatever you were doing. Allow yourself to draw your inner child in a child-like way. No judgements. No "I can't draw". Just let whatever comes come. Really have fun with this. There may be some words that come to mind too. (As long as they're words that are expressing his/her true nature, not the experiences they had in life.). This is your opportunity to bring your child to life on paper.

Once you've finished, put your drawing up somewhere that you can see it every day to remind you of that amazing little being who is alive and well and a part of you. Then go out into the world, the two of you, and live life to the full – the life you were meant to live.

CHAPTER SIX - OUR MANY SELVES

"Who's calling the shots?"

Natasha Dern

Take another journey into the inner workings of our mind and we discover what, in counselling terms, are called sub-personalities. Otherwise known as the different voices in our head. Every single one of us has many different voices telling us all sorts of things all day long. Sounds familiar?

I frequently have clients sitting with me and telling me about their inner conflicts. "This part of me says this but another part of me says that. I feel like I'm having a battle with myself." Well, in a way, you are. And if that battle goes on for too long, with too many voices, you can feel as if you're going nuts.

One of the problems is that, alongside thinking that our lives are linear and not realising we have an inner child trooping along with us, we also somehow falsely believe that we should only have one inner voice, one way of seeing things, one point of view. We think that anything else going on in our heads is somehow because we're just muddled and confused and we ought to know better. Other people don't find it difficult to make a decision, move forward in their lives, choose from a menu. What's wrong with us?

Once again a) realising that we all have these different inner voices, b) understanding where they come from and c) knowing what on earth to do with them can make a huge difference in our lives. The

CHAPTER SIX – OUR MANY SELVES

difference between thinking we're going mad, and knowing that we're completely normal and able to handle the din. The difference between being stuck and unable to move forward in our lives because of the conflicting opinions of this noisy crowd, and being able to hear above the din so we can make decisions that are truly right for us. The difference between feeling constantly at the beck and call of this bunch of dwellers-between-our-ears, and more calmly and clearly making progress in our lives.

So firstly, let's have a look at what these voices actually are. Well, putting it very simply (and I like simple) they've arrived through a mixture of things that other people have told us, things that we've told ourselves and our early experiences in life. Let's once again go back to our bright and shiny newborn selves. This is the point at which we are a clean slate. No opinions, attitudes, beliefs written on our internal blackboard as yet (shows how old I am. It should be a whiteboard, of course!). But then, as we go through life, we inevitably interact with the world around us and, alongside soaking up beliefs and taking on board the 'voices' of others, we also react and respond to the situations we find ourselves in by creating different facets to our personality to cope with them.

For example, you might have had a parent who was very fearful around money, never believing that there would be enough. That parent might have constantly been saying things like, "Money doesn't grow on trees. Do you know how hard I have to work for…? We'll never be able to afford X." This parent might have always been 'saving for a rainy day' (so many of those in the UK. How does anyone ever save anything?) and never allowing themselves to enjoy the pleasure of spending money on something frivolous or luxurious. Let's call this sub-personality Scrooge.

At this point I want to make the distinction between actually having very little money and being fearful around money. Some of you will have had parents who actually had very little money but never made you feel the lack of it and lived with an attitude of abundance. On the other hand, there will be those of you whose parents did have more than enough money but always made you very conscious of the difficulty of acquiring it and the need to hold onto it very tightly when you did have it. I digress a little but money is such a complex and fascinating topic. Worth a book on its own. Also, it's very likely that at least some, if not all, of your current attitudes to money came from your childhood so it's really important to be aware of what the messages were if you're having any difficulties at all around financial abundance.

So fast-forward thirty years and you long to buy that new Audi A5 convertible (OK, I confess, *I* long to buy that new Audi A5 convertible!) and you hear one voice saying, "You can afford it. You deserve it. Go for it." Then you hear another voice saying, "That's really extravagant. Shouldn't you be saving this money/putting it towards your pension/keeping it in a pot under the bed in case the roof falls in?" You might also have developed a Scrooge facet to your personality which finds it hard to let go of money once you have it

CHAPTER SIX – OUR MANY SELVES

(because there might not be any more coming your way).

I'm now going to expand on this example to give you greater understanding of just how crowded this internal show can become. Enter one of the lead characters in many people's heads – The Inner Critic. Recognise this one?

I certainly do! It's a character who could well have stopped me writing this book. To explain, my mother was a highly successful TV scriptwriter and for a while I tried to follow in her footsteps. However, it reached the stage where every 'and' or 'but' that I wrote would be evaluated by my Inner Critic and deemed to be not as good as my mother's. What a great example of stifling my own unique creativity and allowing my Inner Critic to rule the show. But I knew even then that one day I would come back to writing something from my heart which would be more important than listening to my Inner Critic.

Now either you had a parent who was actually very critical of you: "You got 9 out of 10, could have done better." Or you set up your own expectations of yourself and deemed yourself to have failed ("My best friend has got into that school so why didn't I?"). Often our Inner Critic is a combination of both – a parent's (adult authority figure's) voice and our own self-judgement.

Talking of which, let's bring another lead character – The Judge – into the show too. When we're small, we simply do things. That's it. We think of something. We do it. Then we do something else. As we grow older, our actions are assessed. "What about if you'd done this rather than that? Might things have worked out better then?" And so we learn to judge the things we do, the actions we take and the decisions we make. Are we getting it right or wrong? And we develop an inner voice, that of The Judge, who sets up in court somewhere very close to one or other of our ears and constantly judges whatever we do. How free do you think we feel to make choices and decisions when we've got an Inner Judge constantly yammering away at us?

The cast of characters grows as we go through our childhood into adolescence depending on the people, situations and experiences we encounter. The problem is that we then think that they're us. Well, they are part of us in the sense that they exist in our heads but they're not actually the essence, the truth, the heart of us. They're like barnacles sticking to a rock (let's imagine that rock to be a diamond).

Once we start to be more aware of these inner voices – from a place of curiosity and interest rather than becoming dizzy through listening to them – we realise that we have many of them. For example, as women we usually like to think of ourselves as 'nice' people but often we've got a waspish inner Bitch lurking in there somewhere. Rather than "Does my bum look big in this?" she's thinking, "Boy, does her bum look big in that!"

That's another thing about this cast of characters – not only do they judge and criticize you but they do the same to others too. "Who do they think they are? Too big for their boots. They spend money like it was going out of fashion." And on and on. Not a moment's peace!

Some other common sub-personalities are The Worrier (recognise either/both of your parents here?); The Controller; The People

CHAPTER SIX – OUR MANY SELVES

Pleaser; The Procrastinator; The Loser (It's OK for everyone else but it's never going to work out for me); The Rescuer; The Rebel…. Any of these ringing some very familiar and uncomfortable bells?

I'll give you an example from my own life. My father was highly critical of my mother and my brother. (Sadly the person he was most critical of was himself.) Now he was never actually critical of me (I was his Princess, a wonderful but guilt-inducing position to hold in the family). However, I grew up in an atmosphere of criticism and can well remember how deeply it affected the other two members of my immediate family. Even though I wasn't the one being criticized, I lived around that energy of criticism. So as the years went by I developed my own Inner Critic, who would be very much alive and well today if I hadn't learnt how to recognise and handle him (not always but a lot of the time these days).

A great way of telling whether you are thinking/feeling from the core of your being or whether one of your sub-personalities is running the show for you is noticing how much the words 'should' and 'ought' appear. Those two words are the whips belonging to The Inner Critic and The Judge. "You should be doing better." "You ought to have got it right by now." "You shouldn't be so upset." "You oughtn't to think you're something special." If left unchecked, these shoulds and oughts can run riot in our lives and, without realising it, we find ourselves ruled by them. The more we do that, the more out of touch with ourselves we become. The voice of that self, that part of us that wants to live an inspired, fulfilling, rewarding life gets drowned out by this list of rules and regulations that are being imposed on us from within.

My client, Sally, was a high-flying executive with a large team to manage. When she came to me she was suffering from acute stress through working in a high-pressure and challenging business environment. Understandable, you may say, to feel stressed in such a workplace.

However, on further exploration we discovered that one of the main reasons for her feeling so stressed was that she felt she had to control everything and everyone in her team. No one was allowed to do anything without getting her permission, which was not only driving her team members nuts (reading between the lines) but was slowly driving her nuts too.

We then delved deeper still and Sally started to tell me about her childhood. She became quite tearful when she began talking about her parents' divorce when she was seven. It had been a bitter divorce and her parents had engaged in a tug-of-war with Sally as the prize. She had felt completely out of control, torn between both parents with no power to make any choices – and her parents were too fixated in their battle to think about asking her. In talking to me she recognised that from that age she had created The Controller. (Please understand that this isn't a conscious decision which we make. It's our subconscious trying to protect us.) The Controller was her way of making sure that she was never out of control of anything in her life again. It was trying to protect her from ever experiencing those traumatic and painful feelings of powerlessness and confusion. And here is a valuable clue as

CHAPTER SIX – OUR MANY SELVES

to how to deal with our sub-personalities. It (The Controller) thought it was trying to help her.

Once The Controller came to light, Sally began to realise that she was living her life based on an experience from long ago and that now, as an adult, she could trust that she didn't need to be in control in the same way. She went back to work recognising that it was an impossible challenge to try to control everything, allowing her team more freedom and autonomy and relaxing into letting life flow more instead of holding on tightly to imaginary reins.

So what *do* we do with these different aspects of our personality? How do we handle the chattering crowd in our head to get some peace, some perspective and make wise choices that are right for us?

Firstly, it's really important to recognise that we (at the core of our being) are not them. They have come crowding in around us until we can't hear ourselves think. In counselling terms we use the word 'dis-identification' to explain the process of no longer completely identifying with these characters but stepping back so that we can observe them rather than being lost in the crowd. I like to use the image of being a conductor of an orchestra. Imagine your core, essential self (the part of you that truly knows what is best for your happiness and fulfillment) as being the conductor. Your sub-personalities are the different members of that orchestra and you're aiming to be able to request them to perform or be silent at the flick of your baton.

But why would we want them there at all, these pesky characters?

Well, that goes back to what I was saying earlier about them thinking they're trying to help us. Each and every sub-personality believes it has a valuable role to play in keeping you on the straight and narrow, out of harm's way and especially in keeping you from getting hurt.

Let me give you examples from those sub-personalities mentioned earlier.

Scrooge – is trying to protect you from running out of money.

The problem is that the more you hold onto money and fear the lack of it, the more you restrict the flow of money into your life and the more your life is ruled by fear of not having enough. You never get to experience feelings of abundance, generosity and ease around money – both giving and receiving – which are hugely important parts of living a luscious life.

The Inner Critic – thinks that through criticizing you, you will try harder, do better and then one day you'll be good enough and win that gold star.

The problem is that it's actually a never-ending spiral. The harder you try, the more The Critic wants from you. Still not quite good enough. Until in the end you can't bear to try any more because you feel criticized to death (and, in a way The Critic is killing your spirit – not literally because that's impossible but it certainly feels like it). Also, you know now, (because you've read the earlier chapter on The Collective Myth of Not Good Enough, right?) that this is not the way to feel good about yourself.

The Judge – thinks that if it judges everything you say and do then you'll stand a better chance of 'getting it right' – and so make a success of your life.

The problem with this is that there's no such thing as 'getting it right'. Getting it right is a similar problem to being good enough. Both ideas are based on some undefined external examining board whose job it is to tick your exam paper or fail you if you underperform. The ONLY (and I'm putting that in capitals because it's SO important to understand this) way we can be good enough and get it right is by listening to our own internal guiding forces, those quiet whispering voices which actually speak with increasing volume the more we shush those sub-personalities. Be quiet. I want to hear my SELF speak.

The Worrier – thinks that if only it anticipates and worries about every possible eventuality, if only it has every potential crisis covered, then you'll be safe.

There are two fairly obvious problems here. The first is that it's impossible to cover every potential future disaster – so we end up worrying even more in case there are some that we've missed. The second problem is that worrying doesn't make the slightest bit of difference, (let me differentiate here between worrying and constructively thinking of a solution to a problem) especially as we mostly worry about things we have no control over. "Will the plane crash?" "Will it rain tomorrow when we've planned a day out?" "Will my daughter get the A level grades she needs?" Actually worrying does make a difference – it makes things worse. Once you're caught in the worry spiral, other worries are magnetically attracted to that spiral like iron filings attract to one another.

The Controller – thinks that if it could only get everything under control then you'll be able to relax and feel safe. You'll know that you're in control of the world rather than the world controlling you. (The Controller can have a far-reaching impact on our lives. Or, to put it another way, it can wreak huge havoc on our lives. It often makes its presence felt if you've been abused as a child or experienced any kind of particularly difficult and painful childhood where you felt as though you had no control at all – as my client, Sally, did in my earlier example. And so The Controller will subsequently do its damndest to never let you experience those feelings again. Its grip will often manifest in the shape of an eating disorder – either anorexia or bulimia – completely controlling what we do or don't eat. Or overeating, where the control being exercised is different. That's more about 'I can eat what I want, when I want and no one's going to stop me'.)

The problem with this is of course that we can't control everything around us and often, the more we try to control, the more things feel as though they're falling apart – or at least out of control. Then we feel even worse and The Controller increases its grip even further. Yet another never-ending spiral.

The People Pleaser – thinks that if only you can always say and do what other people want – then you'll be liked/loved. This sub-personality often develops in children whose parents were preoccupied with other stuff, who didn't pay them much attention, or were perhaps too involved in the drama of their relationship to give their children what they needed. So as children we begin to think that if only we could be the way our parents want us to be (get it right) then we'll be loved and acknowledged and heard and seen – everything that we all want.

The problem with this is we end up trying to be all things to all people, becoming a watered-down, wishy-washy version of ourselves which is at times, quite frankly, irritating. Who are the people you're most attracted to? Isn't it those people who, somehow or other, (probably because they either had fabulous parents or paid lots of money to a great therapist!) have the courage to be themselves. You can tell, can't you? They somehow radiate 'them'. They may be bluntly honest at times – but you forgive them. They may be very different from you – but you love being around them. The irony is that the way to be really truly loved (what the People Pleaser most wants) is to be really and truly yourself.

The Procrastinator – thinks that if only it can prevent you from actually *doing* things then it will protect you from emotional pain of any kind – such as fear (if you make that call); rejection (if you write that book and no one wants to publish it); paying that pile of bills (dealing with reality/facing the possibility that there isn't enough money to pay them/experiencing overwhelm at the size of the pile). We often call ourselves lazy but I think it's frequently The Procrastinator at work pulling us in the opposite direction from the one that would really benefit us. Or finding any number of reasons or distractions for not doing what we say we're going to.

The problem with The Procrastinator's thinking is that it's actually getting you to avoid your own life and all the many facets of it that could lead to greater opportunities and to you feeling good about yourself. "I made the call and she does want to go out for a drink." "I'm beyond thrilled. My book has been accepted by a publisher." "I did it! I paid those bills. What a relief."

Of course the above scenarios may not turn out as well as I've described (that's the beauty of writing a book. You can make things turn out however you want!). But even so, to learn to deal with e.g. fear, rejection, current reality is far, far more empowering and growth-ful than the ostrich approach favoured by The Procrastinator.

The Loser – wants you to believe that success and The Good Life are only for other people. He wants you to think that it's not even really worth you trying as nothing works out for you. The reason for this is if you adopt that attitude and so never try to achieve much in life then of course you can't risk failure or rejection. Aim low to avoid disappointment.

The problem with this is that your whole life becomes one big disappointment and that's no way for anyone to live now, is it?

The Rescuer – wants you to think that your role in life is to go about 'rescuing' people. This can be seen with people who stick with their alcoholic/abusive partners because someone needs to look after them.

Or people who always seem to attract friends with problems. Well, someone has to be their shoulder to lean on. If you do all these things, The Rescuer will tell you, that proves you're a valuable, worthwhile person. It gives you a right to exist.

The problem with this is rescuing never makes you feel worthwhile. You end up getting more and more sucked into the rescuing, which is draining and anyway, it rarely works for the person being rescued. They just come to rely on you more and more or become increasingly abusive towards you and, rather than feeling valuable, you can easily end up feeling worthless – the very feeling you were trying to avoid.

The Rebel – wants you to think that you need to do life your way – and only your way. You are not to listen to anyone else – understand – because it's vital to live life on your terms. That'll show 'em. The Rebel usually develops because of being over-controlled. After so much 'You will do this' often a 'Like hell I will' erupts and The Rebel is born.

The problem with this is that we can carry on rebelling long after we've made our point. Many adults operate largely from their Rebel, causing chaos and havoc in their personal and professional lives because they're unable to listen to anyone else's point of view.

Well, as you've probably gathered by now there are many different types of sub-personalities (London Philharmonic has got nothing on the size of this orchestra). I just wanted to give you a guided tour of a few of the more common sub-personalities for you to get the idea and probably identify with one or two (or three?) of them.

The concert can become particularly raucous when several sub-personalities want to 'play their tune' at the same time. That's when you retire to bed with a migraine.

So now you know about these inner guests, what can you do about them? Much as you might want to get rid of them, that's not the answer. That only re-starts the inner battle that you're trying to subdue. There are several steps.

1. Become aware of the fact that they exist.

2. Start to recognise the different voices and acknowledge which of them is having their say.

3. Recognise that they think they're trying to help you in their misguided way. They're not the enemy within but were formed, for the most part, when you were very young and they were doing their very best to look after and protect you.

4. Begin to have a 'conversation' with them (although probably not in the middle of the supermarket) to let them know that you understand why they're there but that you're an adult now and you can truly take care of yourself. But make sure to let them know that you appreciate their presence in your life and that you know they were only trying to help you.

5. Self-mastery starts to come when you can see that each sub-personality still does have something valuable to offer you and you make use of that. For example: The Controller can come in when it's important and useful to have things organised and under control (say,

if you're planning for an important meeting). Scrooge can work with you to help you treat money respectfully. The Critic can be brought in to help you do your best with a piece of work.

The aim is to recognise that YOU are the conductor, this is YOUR orchestra and to become skillful in the use of that baton.

Exercise:

Have fun with this....

1. Write down a list of as many of your sub-personalities as you can identify – giving them all names. (These can be anything, by the way. I have a client who calls one of her sub-personalities 'Fred' or they can be 'The Mad Monk', 'The Crabby Critic', 'The Rebel Without a Cause'... As long as it means something to you.) Leave a gap under each sub-personality. You're going to come back to it.

2. In those gaps, start to identify when you think the sub-personality was formed and what it was there to do. How did it think it was helping you?

3. Get out your crayons and draw a cartoon version of each sub-personality. Really let yourself have fun with this one and don't censor anything you want to draw (or write) about each sub-personality. This isn't about being good at drawing, it's about creating an image of each sub-personality to help you to separate yourself from 'it'. The more instantly you can visualize what 'it' looks like, the more quickly you can remember that it isn't you.

4. For each sub-personality I'd then like you to say the following sentence......

"Thank you X (Fred/Mad Monk/Crabby Critic) for being in my life and doing your best to help me. However, I now trust myself and the world enough to be at the heart of my own life. I will call on you when I need your support."

5. Close your eyes and imagine yourself standing there conducting your own orchestra. Start to feel how empowering that is. All the various 'instruments' are waiting for you to call the shots. It's your choice and your opportunity to create the music and the life you truly want to live.

CHAPTER SEVEN - HEAVEN AND HELL

"The mind is its own place and, in itself can make a heaven of hell, a hell of heaven."

John Milton

Don't worry, I'm not suddenly about to go all fire and brimstone on you. Although there may yet be mention of The Big G (otherwise known as God). This is about the heaven and hell that exist in our own minds. Perhaps that's the only place where heaven and hell have ever really existed – however they've been described.

This 'heaven and hell' idea is such a powerful concept once you really get it. It can almost change your life in an instant. Or certainly change how you feel about your life.

The traditional, generally accepted version of how the world works is that something good happens to us and we respond positively i.e. we feel good. Something bad happens to us and we respond negatively i.e. we feel bad. That's completely logical. Makes sense, right?

However, there are two fundamental flaws in this way of thinking. A way of thinking that makes us feel out of control of our own lives, a victim of circumstance and as though we're simply standing there being a punch-bag for whatever blows life throws at us.

The first is the initial labelling of things as 'good' or 'bad'. We really don't ultimately know what's good or bad for us. Something that can seem bad at the time may turn out to be absolutely in our best interests.

Have you heard the story of the farmer, his son and his horse?

Many years ago in a village lived a poor farmer and his son. His only material possession, apart from the land and a small hut, was a horse.

One day the horse ran away, leaving the man with no animal with which to work the land.

His neighbours came round to commiserate with him on the bad news.

"Bad news, good news. Who's to say?" replied the farmer.

A week later the horse returned to its stable, bringing with it a beautiful mare. Another horse to till the land.

The village inhabitants came to congratulate the farmer on the good news.

"Good news, bad news. Who's to say?" replied the farmer.

A month later the farmer's son decided to break the mare in. However, the animal bucked wildly and threw the boy off. The boy fell awkwardly and broke his leg.

The neighbours once again came round and commiserated on the bad news.

"Bad news, good news. Who's to say?" was the farmer's reply yet again.

CHAPTER SEVEN – HEAVEN AND HELL

A few months went by and war was declared. All healthy young men were enlisted and sent to war. The farmer's son was not recruited as his leg hadn't mended yet. None of the young men came back alive.

That story, for me, is a very graphic way of illustrating that we never really know how something will unfold in our lives at the moment that it happens.

A simple illustration from my own life comes from the time when I had my heart set on buying a house in a village in the Cotswolds in Gloucestershire. I had done the classic 'falling in love with a house' thing and desperately wanted to own this house. However, I had reached my financial limit and my final offer still wasn't high enough. The house eventually went to someone who was able to offer just that bit more than me. Emotional devastation followed – did I tell you about my Drama Queen sub-personality? (I wasn't the enlightened being then that I am today!) but I eventually picked myself up and found another house that I liked in a different Cotswold village. The builder who came to do the renovation work became my partner for several years (and we're still good friends) and I then met my husband when he came to look at renting the house years later! (Tenants of mine who had lived there in the meantime had got engaged and then married whilst living in the house so it truly was a house where romance flourished – but that's another story!)

I really did learn my lesson from that experience and stopped immediately judging things one way or another. Instead I now try to view what happens to me as 'interesting', as though I'm in some way an observer of my life with curiosity as to what will unfold next. This helps me to not get so sucked into the drama of labelling everything in a positive or negative context. As far as I can, if something seemingly bad happens to me, I ask myself the question "What can I learn from this? What might be the purpose of this happening to me?" rather than "Oh hell, why did this happen to me? Things always go wrong for me." Doesn't feel very empowering when you read it, does it? Well, it's not very empowering when you think it either!

The second flaw in the 'respond badly to bad stuff' way of thinking is this. When we see ourselves and our relationship to the world around us in this way, we then believe that the world around us needs to change in order for us to feel better. If only my family was different, then I'd feel happier, less anxious, more relaxed. If only he'd change, then I would be more loving, less critical, more supportive. If only I enjoyed my work, I'd feel more fulfilled, less depressed, more motivated. If only, if only, if only….

What we singularly fail to realise is there is always something we can do about any situation. We are never helpless victims. The one thing we can always do is choose to change our minds as to how we respond to the world around us. This is the most powerful impact we can make on our lives and the 'good' news (now this *is* good news, believe me!) is that we can do it immediately.

Let me give you some examples:

You are due to go on holiday when you hear there's an air traffic control strike at the airport. You can choose to be distraught, pi***d

CHAPTER SEVEN – HEAVEN AND HELL

off, angry, fed up and frustrated. Or you can decide to look on the bright side – who knows what might have happened if you'd got on that plane, the weather could be better where you are than where you're going, and what on earth is the point of allowing yourself to be pulled down emotionally by something that you can't do anything about anyway? – before swiftly moving on to Plan B.

Your partner is angry and irritable with you. You can decide to be crabby back to him, to give as good as you get and to generally make him pay for being so horrible to you. Or you can decide that he's probably had a bad day, that he's simply taking it out on his nearest and dearest, and give him a hug and offer to give him a massage later on. Which do you think might produce the most desirable outcome for you?! (Note: I'm not talking about partners who are persistently angry and crabby. That requires a different approach. See my client example below.)

Your boss behaves like a bully and is critical and dismissive of you. You can choose to feel put down, rubbish at your job and generally undermined. Or you can choose to see that his bullying is an issue that he has which doesn't have to affect you and remain positive and confident about the work that you do.

There are huge queues at the supermarket and the check-out girl has a wonderful smile. Which are you going to choose to focus on?

Now I know that in all these examples the more enlightened responses are easier said than done. However, as soon as we begin to recognise that we have a choice ('How do I want to feel in/respond to this situation?'), that in itself is hugely liberating. Then, to the degree that we're able to respond in a more emotionally healthy manner, we can (and should) give ourselves a huge pat on the back. We're on the road to freeing ourselves from feeling like victims of the outside world.

We also need to be very aware of the kind of language we use as it can so easily tip us into a negative frame of mind without us realising it. An example of this (which is a particular bugbear of mine) is the way we so freely use the phrase "It was a nightmare". "I was stuck in traffic. It was a nightmare." "We had to wait ages to be served. It was a nightmare. "The gym was so busy. It was a nightmare." Was it really? I don't think so. Young men going to war and not coming back again. Now that's a nightmare.

So really pay attention to the type of language you use because what we tell ourselves has a big impact on us. What kind of impact would you like to make on yourself – and those around you? What kind of language would you need to use to help you to create a life you love?

Here's another everyday example. When asked the question "How are you?" many people reply "Not too bad." I can almost feel myself deflate when I hear that response. (Note I said 'almost' because of course I wouldn't let someone else's words have that kind of impact on me!) Obviously we all do have some days that are better than others but for many people 'not too bad' is a standard response, whatever they're feeling.

Might I be hitting the spot here? It's OK to own up to it if you're a 'not too bad'-er as long as you stop doing it right now. If you're not

CHAPTER SEVEN – HEAVEN AND HELL

having a good day, it's a better idea to say "I'm not having a great day today." But then, when you *are* having a good day, acknowledge that too with an "I'm having a great day today." A one-size-fits-all response of "not too bad" is about as inspiring and uplifting for you (and the recipient) as a soggy tissue.

My client, James, was fed up with being in an unhappy marriage where all he and his wife did was back-stab and point-score. In his sessions with me, he would be frequently critical of his wife, venting his anger about her and the way she behaved towards him.

The sessions were starting to sound like a shopping list of her failings. After going through one such 'list', I asked my client how he felt. "Awful," he replied. "My relationship is a complete mess." I chose my words carefully. "To what degree do you feel awful because of what you've just been saying?" I asked him. "Well, of course I feel awful because of what I've just said," he replied. "If *you* had a wife that…….." I ventured to point out that perhaps part of the reason he felt awful was because of the way he was choosing to see and describe his wife even if some of the things he said were true. I added that if hearing his words made *my* heart sink, what might they be doing to his spirits (let alone those of his wife!)? He started to pay a little more attention.

"What are some of the good things about your wife and your relationship?" I asked. He was stumped at first but then managed to come up with one or two thoughts. I encouraged him to keep going with this until he eventually came up with a surprising number of positive things to say about this harridan of a wife. "Now how do you feel?" I asked. "A bit better," he replied. "And how do you think your wife might respond to you if you chose to appreciate her for something on this list rather than the way you have been talking to one another?" "I think she'd faint!" he replied. I was glad to see that a sense of humour was buried under all the bitterness.

Anyway, James did go away and dip a toe in the water of being nicer to his wife and guess what? (No, she didn't faint!) She backed off a little herself and started being that much nicer to him. Even when his wife went back to her back-stabbing (because she didn't have a counsellor to guide her!), James eventually learnt not to fall back into his old behaviour pattern of returning the blow. He began to recognise that it was his choice how he responded to his wife and that certainly his own life and increasingly his relationship felt so much better for his more positive outlook.

I think there's a wider application to this idea too, which is to choose how we see the world at large. In today's challenging times, I believe that we are being called to make a choice. We can either buy into the 'reality' that we are often confronted with – scarcity, fear, general doom and gloom – or look at what we have intrinsically as human beings. Riches beyond belief – all the love, joy, happiness and inner peace we've ever dreamed of is simply waiting to be discovered. It's our choice.

Either we're part of the problem, and our fearful thoughts help to perpetuate a fearful world. Or we're part of the solution and only choose thoughts that will have a positive impact on ourselves and the world we live in. Let's focus more on seeing the heaven that exists in the world rather than the hell.

So how *do* you want to respond to people and events in your life and in the world? Do you want to create a life that feels uplifting, positive and peaceful or one filled with conflict and woes? When put like that, the choice is pretty obvious, isn't it?

Exercise:

A simple one for this chapter.

I would like you to choose a current situation that you're not happy about. It can be from any aspect of your life – work, relationship, health, family, friends…

Now write about the situation from a negative perspective and really go to town on this. Let every ounce of negative feeling and every niggly, grouchy thought out on paper. Don't hold back. Be bad, be cruel, be really mean and crabby.

Once you've finished, take a moment and notice how you feel.

Next I'd like you to take the same situation and do the opposite. Write about it from the most positive perspective you can find. Really search hard in your heart and mind for every single good thing you can uncover to say about this situation. Don't leave any stone unturned in the quest for golden nuggets buried underneath. Let your goodness flow. Let your inner light shine.

Notice once again how you feel.

Finally, draw your own conclusions!

CHAPTER EIGHT – EGO AND THE HIGHER SELF (otherwise entitled 'Get out of your own way')

"The ego is that ugly little troll that lives under the bridge between your mind and your heart."

Gael Greene

'Ego' is a much-used word these days, isn't it? We talk about people having huge egos but what do we mean? Is this good or bad? Do our egos help or hinder us through our lives?

Well, the short answer is that there is no short answer about what the ego is. The word itself has been around for centuries and originated from Latin: 'ego' being Latin for 'I'. "There. That's simple enough," you might say. "My ego is me. It's who I am." But my whole point in this chapter, as you will see when you read on, is that we are so much more than just our egos.

Psychologists, most notably Freud, used the word ego to describe a part of our selves. If you'd like to read about this, please do, but it's not my intention in this book to explain complex Freudian psychology. Instead I'm going to offer you a hopefully more simple and easy-to-understand description of what I believe the ego to be. And why, as you'll have gathered from the quote I've chosen at the top of the chapter, I don't think it's An Entirely Good Thing!

I believe our ego is our self-protective shell, the part of us that we've built over the years to shield us from perceived harm (all those slings and arrows that others throw at us) and to make us feel better about ourselves. What it's not is the truth about us. The pure unadulterated us-ness that we need to be in touch with in order to thrive in the world.

To explain further, let's once again go back to that beautiful, bonny, bouncing baby that you once were. You come into the world completely raw and naked – in every sense. Your being is untouched by the world. You are not yet influenced or affected by any person or experience. I think this moment of birth and the early months of our lives are the closest we come to being the pure essence of 'us' in this world. (However, even in these very early stages of life, if we don't receive the love, attention and nurturing that we need as a baby then we begin to adapt to and make decisions about ourselves and our environment almost from birth.)

Then, as we continue through life, we're inevitably around people and go through experiences that have an impact on us. As thinking, feeling beings, whatever happens in our world begins to shape how we see and feel about ourselves and others. Our response to the emotional impact that the world has on us is to start to create an ego.

As one of our primary drivers in life is the need for self-protection (both physical and emotional), so one of the earliest facets of our ego to develop is a layer of self-protection. What might this look like? Let me give you an example of a self-protective layer forming in my own life.

When I was a little girl I loved performing. I took drama and

CHAPTER EIGHT – EGO AND THE HIGHER SELF

elocution classes (as they were called in those days) and would relish going up on stage to perform my piece in front of an audience. My little star was well and truly shining as I stood there looking out at a sea of faces. Then, when I was a bit older, I did a modelling course (no idea why now, come to think of it, but there you are) and was being asked questions by someone looking to hire me. Nothing tricky exactly. Something about my 'A' levels, I seem to remember. But I completely dried up. Not a word came out of my mouth as I stood in front of this man. Until off I scuttled, mortified. Fast forward thirty years and if anyone were to ask me how I felt about public speaking, I would say, "Fantastic. For someone else. Definitely not for me. I belong to the 'I'd rather die' brigade." But you see, that was really my ego protecting me from further pain and embarrassment because when I recently addressed this and found the courage to start speaking in public again, guess who popped out? That spangly, starry little girl who had always had a love of public speaking and was once again allowed out to play.

Some more examples of how this ego works.

Let's say you're quite a shy, quiet little being but you then get teased about that – by adults, friends, it doesn't matter who. In order not to get teased any more (because it hurts) you might develop a 'clown' aspect to your personality where you are the centre of attention and make everyone laugh. "What's so wrong with that?" you might say. Obviously you're not doing anyone any harm but over the years you become caught up in this 'clown' part of your ego until you're not able to let go of it, relax and let your quiet, shy self show its face. You're increasingly driven by the need to perform, entertain, be anything other than that part of you that just wants to be quiet and left in peace (for heaven's sake!).

I've had clients come to me feeling completely drained and exhausted. Through gentle exploration and questioning they discover that they have led most of their life protecting themselves by being the life-and-soul and never ever allowing that more vulnerable part of them out into the world. Whilst this has worked to cover up their shyness, it has meant that they've never felt able to be fully and genuinely themselves. They're short changing themselves (and others) by not allowing the real them expression in the world.

Another example of a way that an ego might develop is the child has been bullied at school or at home. Often this has been a deeply traumatic and painful experience which can lead a child to decide (usually sub-consciously, in other words they don't even know that this is a decision they've made) "I'm never ever going to let that happen to me again." Then, in order to protect themselves, as they grow up, the bullied child turns into a bully themselves. If being a bully is the only way not to be bullied (and experience all that pain and trauma again), then that's what has to happen. Someone who has been bullied at school will often try to control and dominate others too (close cousins of bullying), again for fear that if they don't control, they will be controlled themselves. And who is in the driving seat when acting in this way? You guessed it, our ego.

CHAPTER EIGHT – EGO AND THE HIGHER SELF

One more example, just so you really get the hang of this. Suppose your early years weren't great academically. Perhaps you were teased at school, perhaps you had critical parents who made you feel stupid (or at least that was the way it felt at the time), perhaps your siblings were brighter than you. As you've probably gathered by now, one of the ego's roles is to stop you from feeling bad (we don't want any of those frightening, painful, upsetting feelings round here, thank you very much). So as you grow up you become driven by a desire to succeed, to prove everyone wrong (that'll show 'em), to always do better than you're currently doing. The ego believes that if you're doing well then you'll feel better about yourself. (Or of course this early life experience could have the opposite effect and lead to you believing you actually are stupid and consistently under-achieving.)

Once again you may say, "But what's so wrong about having a drive to succeed?" Well, nothing, except that if the ego is in the driving seat then you'll never get to your destination. With the ego navigating, he/she will always want you to travel further, keep going just that bit more – and then you'll feel good about yourself, it whispers encouragingly. But it's lying. Because just when you think you've got there, it will wave the carrot of just one more promotion, just one more qualification. That should do it. And on…and on.

My client Jenny was a brilliant young lawyer. However, when she came to me she was on her knees with self-loathing and exhaustion. To the outside world she was a great, glorious success. But to her she was never quite good enough, always comparing herself to her colleagues, forever chasing the next qualification, studying for the next exam. When we began to explore this she talked about her critical father, who would make her feel stupid if she ever got anything wrong. She grew up feeling that she wasn't allowed to make mistakes when it's crucial that we do allow ourselves to make mistakes and, more damagingly, that she wouldn't have her father's love unless she performed brilliantly.

Jenny began to see that unless she developed new criteria for success – one which was true for her, not based on gaining her father's love – she would never be happy. Together we redefined what success really meant to her – using her knowledge to help others, creating strong and loving relationships, being honest and authentic. Once she was able to do this and let go of the need for her father's love based on her achievements, she felt such relief. She relaxed, redirected her focus and truly thrived.

So if the ego is our outer shell (I imagine something rather brittle and easily broken. We do refer to people's egos as 'fragile', don't we?) what exactly lies inside it? Well, as I mentioned earlier – it's our us-ness. Much like the pearl in the oyster shell, there's something very beautiful lying there waiting if we allow ourselves to open up beyond our shells. Some would call this our higher self – our source of truth, guidance, joy, love, inner peace and everything we truly need to lead a happy and fulfilling life. This is the part of us that has been there from day 1 (although we were too dribbly and concerned with getting fed to

CHAPTER EIGHT – EGO AND THE HIGHER SELF

know it!). It is our core. Our pure, essential essence. It's the truth of who we are.

But we have to a) be aware that the oyster shell exists and b) find the courage to prise it open. Just as the oyster shell was protecting the pearl, so the ego thinks it's protecting us. At times it will battle mightily to remain a closed shell and not allow you access to what lies inside for fear of you getting hurt (or so it thinks).

However, our real pain lies in NOT living our lives from our higher self (or inner self) because essentially we are then allowing ourselves to be dominated by the fearful ego. And if we spend our lives giving way to our egos, then we will remain a small, diminished and down-graded version of ourselves. We will be forever driven by the need to protect ourselves from pain and, paradoxically, forever in pain of some kind or another. It might be a quiet un-named fear humming away in the background or a screaming-out-loud 'I HATE my life' kind of pain, but any which way it's pain that the ego creates.

The more we can recognise that our ego is not who we really are and start to pay attention to our higher selves, the more we will start to live our lives and make our decisions and choices in ways that are so much happier, healthier and more rewarding.

So how do we start to live our lives more from our higher self than our ego? One of the easiest ways is through those decisions and choices. Whenever we make a choice, we are guided essentially by two opposing forces – love and fear. Love is part of our higher self (some may say our higher self IS love). Fear is ego-based. Which do you want to choose?

Some scenarios:

Your good friend was dismissive of your brilliant new business venture when you last met and it hurt (your ego). You've heard she's not feeling great. Your ego says to you: "Don't pick up the phone. She hurt you last time you spoke." It's fearful of you being hurt again and it also wants to pay her back for hurting you. Your higher self might say: "She hurt your feelings. That's no reason to withdraw your love from her. She needs you right now." And so you pick up the phone.

You want to ask the local newspaper to write an article about your brilliant new business venture. Your ego might say: "Don't call. They probably won't be interested. You'll only get rejected." Higher self would say: "Make the call. You're really excited about this venture and want to let everyone know about it. If they say yes, that's great. If they say no, that's fine too." (That's another great thing about the higher self. It doesn't get hurt by seeming rejection. Note: I say 'seeming'. Saying 'no' isn't rejection. It's simply saying 'no'. It's our egos that turn it into rejection and make a big deal out of it.)

Other ways of telling whether you're acting from your ego or your higher self:

* Your ego cares what other people think. Your higher self chooses what feels right to you.

* Your ego will compare you to other people and you'll either come

off better or worse. Your higher self will respect and value you and everyone else for who you are.

* Your ego will tell you you'll feel better if you do this or that. Your higher self will whisper 'do it from a place of feeling good anyway'.

* Your ego will scare you into not doing something. Your higher self will reassure you you'll be OK whatever the outcome.

* Your ego will look for external things – jobs, relationships, possessions – to validate you. Your higher self knows you're fine just the way you are.

A further note about this ego of ours. What about the phrase 'He/she's got a healthy ego'? Is that a good thing – or not? Well, on the surface it sounds like good news. Doesn't it mean that a person feels good about themselves? But if we dig a little deeper, I believe it means that their ego has created several strategies for feeling good, such as believing themselves to be better than others or always wearing designer clothes and driving expensive cars. (I'm not saying there's anything wrong with designer clothes and expensive cars in themselves. It's the way we use them to make ourselves feel better that's the issue here.) In reality, this person has just found excellent strategies for covering up their deeper lack of self-worth. You only need to have read some of the many interviews in 'Hello' magazine to know the truth of this in relation to fame, wealth and success. (Again, nothing wrong with any of those. It just depends on what has led you there and how you relate to these 'worldly trappings' once you have them.)

Whereas when we talk about a person having a healthy sense of self, I believe that means that they acknowledge, value and appreciate their own innate qualities and ability to be a loving, powerful and effective presence in the world. They don't have need of their ego to bolster their sense of self as they have a deep level of self-worth already.

Now in reality, this isn't a black and white situation. For most of us, it's not as though we're either living an ego-led life or a higher self-led life. I think we switch between one state and the other most of the time. So, to go back to the sub-title for this chapter 'Get out of your own way', I think it's more about recognising when our ego is running the show as often as we can and getting out of its over-protective clutches to live in a far better place. The land of the higher self. This takes practice but so does becoming a good tennis player. However, the rewards for spending more time being led by our higher self are even greater than playing that perfect serve.

Exercise:

Choose a decision you currently have to make and firstly describe it from your ego's perspective and then make an ego-led choice. Next describe it from your higher self's perspective and then make a higher self-led choice.

The purpose of this exercise is to help you see more clearly whether it's your ego or your higher self that is running the show. For example: A colleague is launching a new business which is remarkably similar to your own and has asked you to endorse her work.

Your ego might be resentful, judgemental ('why is she copying me?'), fearful that her business might be more successful than yours. Even worse, she might be better than you. You feel reluctant to offer the endorsement even though you know her work is good because you don't want her to be more successful than you. So you tell her you're sorry but you're too busy, or you give her a begrudging, half-hearted endorsement.

Your higher self knows that there is plenty of room in this world for everyone's talents and abilities; in fact, the world needs them all. It knows that everyone has something unique to offer and that she is not a threat to you in any way. Your higher self willingly and enthusiastically gives her an endorsement, whole-heartedly wanting her to do well.

You get the idea? Now off you go…

CHAPTER NINE - YOUR COMFORT ZONE AND BEYOND

"Life begins at the end of your comfort zone."

Neale Donald Walsch

Another often-used phrase is 'comfort zone'. "I know I'm in my comfort zone," people will say, almost as an excuse to themselves for not taking any action. As though by simply acknowledging it, that's enough.

But what is this comfort zone business? How does it work? And why is it important to discuss it? Also, what lies beyond it and how can we navigate our way into these sometimes uncharted waters?

As you're reading through this chapter, it might help to imagine yourself as the centre point of three circles, each with a bigger circumference than the last. The first circle immediately surrounding you is your comfort zone, the next circle surrounding your comfort zone is your uncomfortable zone and the outer circle is your growth zone.

Our comfort zone is where most of us live most of the time, both mentally and physically. It's a place that feels – well – comfortable, familiar, known. So far, I know, that sounds like a good thing but if we stay there too long it can become our whole world and eventually our prison cell.

This comfort zone evolves over the course of our lives as a result of and in reaction to life experiences which haven't exactly been pleasant. Perhaps we tried something once and it didn't work out, leaving us feeling embarrassed and a bit stupid. Maybe we expressed ourselves in a way that was laughed at or we got teased. Perhaps we experimented with something and got shouted at. Or maybe we tried skiing and took a tumble. Each of these outcomes can leave their mark on us and make us feel hesitant to live our lives to the full because it involves risk.

Once again, our ego comes to the rescue and decides to create this cosy little nest (called the comfort zone) where we can stay safe and not risk having any difficult or challenging feelings or any physical hardship. "There. That works nicely," it says. "You're safe in here." The only problem is that the longer we live there, the more difficult it can be to move beyond it. The longer we live there, the more disconnected we become from our power and potential. The longer we live there, the more scared we can become of venturing outside (thus revealing a flaw in the ego's plan by creating the very feelings it's seeking to avoid). And finally, the longer we live there, the more we can forget that there is so much more for us to have, be and do in life just over the comfort zone wall. If you're asking yourself "Is this all there is to life?" then it's very likely that you're in your comfort zone.

Here are some of the things you might find if you go rooting around in your own comfort zone:

Habits – these are simply the way we've thought about and done things for years. We can become stuck in a deep groove with our habits, not questioning whether they're helpful to us or if we need to carry on with them. They can even begin to feel like a part of us. "It's just who I am," clients will say to me. To which I reply: "It's not who you are. It's a habit you acquired along the way. And if you picked it up somewhere, you can put it down too." (I hope that doesn't sound too know-all. It's simply that one of my ultimate aims is to support my clients in knowing who they are as opposed to who they believe themselves to be.)

Your current level of self-worth – this becomes most apparent when we consider doing something that might be outside our comfort zone. Perhaps we want to apply for a promotion or go on a dating website or run a marathon. If you're considering doing anything new and that little voice in your head pipes up "But you don't have what it takes" or "You're not good enough to do that" or "Who would want you?" then you're being held back by the way you feel about yourself. The little voice leaps in (all too quickly at times, have you noticed?) to persuade you not to take any action. "Stay here where it's nice and familiar," it says. "No harm can come to you in here." However, none of what your heart really longs for lives in the comfort zone either.

Fear – all our fears huddle together in the comfort zone, whispering and conspiring to keep us from taking any risks. Have you noticed yourself having an inspired thought and then immediately your internal voice replies, "But you might fail or you might look stupid or, or, or…" Now I'm not saying that fear disappears once you step beyond your comfort zone. At times it will intensify (more of that later). But the comfort zone is the place where we allow our fears to stop us from living life the way we'd really like to, if only we weren't afraid.

Limiting beliefs – these pop up the moment we think about trying something new or doing something different in our lives. You'll find yourself thinking along these lines: "But someone like me can't do X or Y." I don't have what it takes." Sound familiar? If we don't understand that we are simply listening to a belief we've bought into, we can easily fall into the trap of replying, "Yes, you're right. I can't do that." Once again, you've been saved from possible pain – and a rich and fulfilling life.

Now I'm not saying that being in our comfort zone is always a bad thing. There are times in our lives when we need to recharge, relax and not push ourselves too hard. If we've been ill, for example, or been through a bereavement or divorce or any challenging life experience, then we need to be in a familiar place for a while. But use your comfort zone as a safe harbour to come back to and rest awhile rather than pitching a life-long anchor there.

So what happens if we choose to step outside our comfort zone and decide to do something new, risky or challenging? Initially we may find ourselves in an area I'll call:

The Uncomfortable Zone – for obvious reasons!

This is the territory beyond the comfort zone. It can feel unfamiliar and at times downright scary. But it's important to understand what we might be coming up against in the uncomfortable zone so that we can see it's just part of a process we're going through and, hopefully, I'll convince you that it's worth it in order to wade through this to the growth zone.

As Rhonda Britten says in her book 'Fearless Living', some of the things you might come up against are:

Believing messages from the past. A loud voice might be shouting in your ear: "Why open yourself up to looking stupid? You know you're no good at public speaking." Or "What on earth convinced you that you could do this? You've never been business-minded. What were you thinking?" This is essentially the voice of your now-familiar adversary – fear.

Often when we're on the way to something bigger and better for us, our fears will be even more potent than they've ever been. Fear is making one last desperate attempt to catch you in its net and haul you back to the safety of the comfort zone. It will use any wiles it can to achieve its aim, which is to stop you from whatever you're doing that feels risky.

The important message here (and this is oh so important) is not to allow these feelings to make you scamper back to the comfort zone. The aim is to be able to say "OK, I'm feeling afraid but that's no reason to turn back." If you keep going, I promise you that your fear will eventually lose its power over you. It will shrink from being a fire-breathing monster (OK, that's a pretty big fear!) to a pesky little mouse nibbling at your trouser leg. It's not that your fear will necessarily disappear (though it may). It's just that you start paying less attention to it as you become more focused on where you want to get to and begin to experience the benefits of heading there.

Feeling like a fake. When we embark on a new course of action it can sometimes feel like we're not really being 'us', that we're being phony.

I've frequently had clients saying to me: "I'm scared that they're going to find me out one day." I sometimes have an inner smile when I hear this because I have a vision of a group of respected senior level managers (which many of my clients are) all leaving a high-powered meeting, walking round the corner and breathing a sigh of relief: "Phew, wasn't found out that time!" And I do think the feeling is as common as that – if we cared to admit it.

To take this idea a stage further, I think that the real issue is not about being found out but about taking ourselves seriously, recognising that we do actually have the talents and abilities that we think we're just pretending to have.

So this phony feeling is just the time lag between growing out of your old skin and growing into your new skin. There's no such thing as a static 'you'. We're all beings of immense possibility and potential. Who you are at any one time is only a snapshot at that time.

Feeling lost. When we're in our uncomfortable zone this is new territory so it can bring up feelings of not knowing quite how to behave or respond. "What should I do next? Where should I go? How do I do this?" Everything is so unfamiliar.

But this is simply part of the path from A (your comfort zone) to B (your growth zone). It's natural, normal and not something to be defeated by.

Imagine you're going on a car journey (before SatNavs) from your comfortable home to the north of Scotland (unless you already live in the north of Scotland in which case use your imagination!). You know it's probably going to be quite a long journey and you really want to go but you're not sure of the route. You try your best to read the map but get lost several times. There are moments when you wish that you hadn't even bothered to leave your safe, cosy, familiar home. But eventually you arrive in those Scottish Highlands and there's a friendly welcome waiting for you at your hotel. As you sip a glass of wine and look out over a stunning loch you relax contentedly and think to yourself, "I'm so glad I made the journey. It was well worth the effort – including getting lost at times."

It's much the same when we decide to travel from a familiar emotional place to somewhere new. We need to accept that feeling lost is part of the journey and hold onto the image of that metaphorical glass of wine and stunning view at the end.

Not that this really is the end of your journey because there's another zone beyond the uncomfortable zone. And this is what makes it all worthwhile.

This is your Growth Zone.

This is the place where you get to experience growth (obviously!);

CHAPTER NINE – YOUR COMFORT ZONE AND BEYOND

fulfillment; a sense of achievement; feeling 'alive'; more energy and vitality; a sense of purpose; an expanded vision of who you are and what you can achieve; a buzz of excitement. Definitely worth the journey.

Then, after a while, this place becomes our new comfort zone and the process continues, should we choose it.

Now this might all sound a bit daunting but, if we think about it, we've been through this cycle many times in our lives (without necessarily realising it) from an early age. Starting school; going on your first date; starting your first job; beginning again after a relationship breakup; starting a new business; running your first marathon. All of these experiences begin with us not knowing how to, encountering doubts and fears (if you're anything like me) and then overcoming them, learning more about yourself in the process and realising that actually you CAN do it.

All I'm doing in writing about this is to encourage you to go through the cycle in a more conscious way, recognising which zone you're in and using that information for your growth and fulfillment.

I also realise that in reality this isn't such a black and white process. We often vacillate between the zones depending on the day or (again if you're like me) the hour. However, I think it's still helpful to recognise where we are emotionally at any given time, particularly if it's not where we want to be!

My most recent experience of this was being asked to do a one hour live radio interview with a bit of agony-aunt-ing thrown in. The phone call inviting me on the programme sent me hurtling into my uncomfortable zone but I knew when I was asked that the only answer to give was "Yes." (I'd obviously been reading my book!) In the days leading up to the interview I was worried about sounding stupid, concerned about responding like a 'proper' agony aunt (rather than faking it) and anxious that I didn't really know how to do this – it was all new to me. Yes, I was in grade A, 5 star uncomfortable zone territory.

However, I went ahead with it and quickly realised, as I was sitting in the radio studio, that I was loving it. I came out of that studio on a complete high, firstly for having survived but more than that I felt as though I'd just discovered a new part of myself and felt somehow expanded and more alive as a result. Gold star for getting to the growth zone.

It's enormously rewarding to be supporting, guiding and (at times) cajoling my clients into their growth zones too.

Frances had been in a deeply unhappy and abusive marriage for many years. When she came to see me she was anxious, depressed and couldn't see much that was good about life. However, she was clinging on to her marriage because, awful as it was, the alternative seemed terrifying. She had been married for so long that she didn't think she could cope by herself. Plus her self-esteem had taken a real battering over the years.

Through the course of our work together, Frances came to see that

CHAPTER NINE – YOUR COMFORT ZONE AND BEYOND

uncomfortable though it was (to put it mildly) she was actually in her comfort zone. Her misery and despair were familiar. Anything different was new territory. However, she began to understand that life (her Inner Self) was calling her to face her fear and step into the uncomfortable zone. So, taking a huge leap of faith, she finally brought her marriage to an end.

Initially Frances experienced an enormous sense of relief but then the doubts set in. "Will I cope on my own? Who would ever want me?" She also noticed how lost she felt. "This is all so new and daunting. I don't know how to live a single life."

It felt to Frances like sink or swim. However, as I guided her through those stormy waters (she was actually a pretty good swimmer, she just didn't recognise it), she gradually noticed that the sea was getting calmer and there were no sharks around (other than those in her imagination) and finally she climbed ashore in the Growth Zone.

Frances is now happily single, dating but in no hurry to meet her 'Mr Right', relaxed and feeling very proud of herself for having found the courage and stuck with it to create the life that she's living today.

Hopefully by outlining the three different stages of emotional territory that we live in, you are now more able to identify where you're currently hanging out. If it's the comfort zone, you're with most of the human race – only now you know it. (And if you need to rest there awhile right now then enjoy the break, put your feet up and make the most of it.) There's no judgement or criticism implied. I'm simply asking the question "What do you want? What do you really really want?" and mostly the answer isn't in that comfort zone.

In the words of Neale Donald Walsch: "Life begins at the end of your comfort zone."

If you're currently in your uncomfortable zone, let me throw out an imaginary lifebelt to you with the words 'YOU WILL GET THROUGH THIS' printed on it. There. Wrap that around you – body, mind and spirit – and know that you're aiming for foreign shores but when you get there you will be greeted with a large cocktail complete with paper umbrella and glacé cherry on a stick (anyone else old enough to remember those?) and a huge cheer from your fellow growth zoners.

And if you're already in your growth zone, give yourself a huge cheer. I hope you're really taking the time to enjoy the rewards of being here and acknowledging and appreciating yourself for everything it's taken to get to this place.

Finally in this chapter I'm going to give you a list of 'ingredients' that would be helpful for you to pack in your backpack for the journey:

Courage, faith, trust, belief (that there's more *for* you and more *to* you and that you CAN do it), patience, perseverance, determination, humour and an ability to ask for help. Add to this a huge dollop of self-appreciation as you travel on your way.

(Apologies if there are too many nautical references here. My husband's obsession with the sea is rubbing off on me!)

CHAPTER NINE – YOUR COMFORT ZONE AND BEYOND

Exercise:

N.B. This exercise is to be done with compassion for yourself. No self-judgement allowed!

Draw your own Comfort Zone chart with the three different zones marked.

Now I'd like you to take some time and sit quietly with your eyes closed (having read this first!) and allow yourself to think about an area of your life that you're really challenged by right now. What's on your mind the most? Is it your home life, your work, your relationships, your health, your social life?

Once you've chosen an aspect of your life to focus on, bring to mind the three zones and decide which zone you're in for this particular part of your life. If you're in the comfort zone, start to think about some of the things you're experiencing there e.g. feeling stuck, anxious, bored, afraid. (If you're already in your uncomfortable zone, well done for taking that first leap.)

Now think about what it might feel like if you were to take a leap of faith and move into your uncomfortable zone. What feelings might arise there? Perhaps confusion, unfamiliarity, self-doubt, what am I doing this for? (Again, if you're already in your uncomfortable zone, be honest with yourself about what you're experiencing there.)

And finally think about how you would feel if you were to move into your growth zone – maybe excited, fulfilled, I CAN do it, a sense of self-worth and generally in a great place.

Now open your eyes and write down those feelings in the appropriate zone.

Take some time to look at the chart you've created. You've outlined a map of your feelings, taking you from where you are to where you want to be. You've been honest with yourself about where you are, named some of the feelings you're likely to experience along the way and described a goal to aim for i.e. the way you'd like to feel.

All you need to do now is read Chapter 10!

CHAPTER TEN – DECIDE WHAT YOU WANT AND DO IT

"Many people die with their music still in them. Why is this so? Too often it is because they are always getting ready to live. Before they know it, time runs out."

Oliver Wendell Holmes, former U.S. Supreme Court Justice

Sounds obvious and simple, doesn't it? Decide what you want and do it. But how many of us know what we want in the first place, let alone take the steps to do something about it? Somehow there's a presumption that we should all know what we want in life. Everyone else seems to – right? Wrong. There are so many people who are just wandering through life with no particular aim or direction, just getting by day after day. (And if I've hit a nerve, my apologies but I'm glad too, because this needs to be brought to your attention!)

Having greater awareness and understanding of ourselves (as I hope you're gaining through reading this book so far) is hugely important. It's the foundation stone for everything else. But if we just sit at home twiddling our thumbs and reflecting on our new-found ability to understand ourselves, we're not going to actually change much in our lives. I want to encourage you to take all the information I've given you and apply it as you go about creating more of what you want in your life. So what *do* you want?

An exercise I ask people to do in my BBB Club course (which stands for Bigger Better Bolder) is this: Two people sit opposite one another and for five minutes one person asks the other one question: "What do you want?" over and over again. The other person answers with whatever comes into their head. "A pair of purple shoes; lunch; inner peace; a new kitchen; a holiday; self-belief; more time to relax; a dog…" You get the idea. There are no wrong answers. Then the partners swap roles and do it all over again.

This was an exercise I first experienced on a personal development seminar called Insight many years ago. As an atheist at the time, to my complete astonishment I found myself uttering the word "God" and bursting into tears.

It was in that one ten minute exercise that I realised ('felt with all my heart' would be a more appropriate way of describing it) that I was a spiritual being and wanted a connection with God, rather than proudly calling myself an atheist and seeing anyone who had any spiritual/religious beliefs as weak.

This one simple exercise can be oh so powerful. Try it with a friend but make sure it's someone with whom you feel able to say anything that pops out of your mouth because you too might be surprised!

One of the things that people frequently report is how difficult they find the exercise, how hard it is to think about what they want – what they truly, truly want.

But the point is – if *you* don't decide, who *is* going to? It can be all too easy to cruise (or in many cases crawl) through life waiting for

CHAPTER TEN – DECIDE WHAT YOU WANT AND DO IT

something to happen one day. As they say, "Life isn't a dress rehearsal," and as I ask on my website: "How do you want to live yours?"

When we say we don't know what we want, I think it's partly because we want someone else to come along and make the decision for us, some properly adult person who will make a good decision for us. No, even better, the *right* decision. Perhaps for many of us not making decisions about our lives feels better than making a decision and getting it wrong. But what if there was no 'getting it wrong'? I prefer to think of making choices rather than decisions. If I make choice A, it leads me down path A. If I make choice B, it leads me down path B. No right or wrong. Just different paths with different outcomes and life experiences (learning) along the way.

So for those of you who are drifty-dreamers, perhaps you're getting the message that it really is important to take matters into your own hands and decide what you damn well want. However, that alone isn't enough. For example, you might decide: "OK, I want a holiday." But that isn't going to get you very far. A holiday……where, when, who with? Now these questions might seem obvious but if you think about it, don't we often do a similar thing with other areas of our lives, other probably more important areas? We might say 'I want a better job' or 'I want to live by the sea'. The same questions apply – what exactly are you looking for?

In other words, it's important to set goals, and to be really clear about what exactly you want and when you want it by.

There's a useful tool called a SMART goal to help with goal setting. SMART is an acronym for:

S = Specific

e.g. I want to go on holiday to Kanuhura in the Maldives with my husband for a fortnight.

M = Measurable

e.g. I will know when I've achieved this goal. I'll be bronzed, relaxed and £10,000 poorer!

A = Achievable

e.g. I can book the flight and hotel. No problem.

R = Realistic

e.g. Not right now. I need to have £10,000 saved so will open a bank account especially for my holiday immediately.

T = Time specific

e.g. For a fortnight departing next Valentine's Day.

Now it may be that you have a huge goal, for example to move to another country. One of the things that most often happens when we have a goal this big is that it can seem overwhelming and then what do we do? We do nothing. It's just all too big and scary. In order not to feel overwhelmed, we need to break our big goals down into smaller steps (sometimes called 'chunking it down') that do feel manageable and achievable. So moving to another country might require research into house prices in the country you've chosen, looking at employment or business opportunities, setting up a bank account to save for this move, checking out visa requirements. All of these smaller steps, if followed, will take you closer and closer to your end goal. It's important to remember that no matter how much anyone has achieved (especially the people you look at and think 'I couldn't do that'), they've all got there step by step. So what is your first step going to be?

Ahh humm, I have to hold my hand up and be honest here and admit that I'm a fairly recent convert to this way of thinking. Yes, I'm a trained life-coach and yes, I've been working on goal-setting with my clients for years but somehow I had let myself off the hook on this one. Somehow, to my warped way of thinking (on this subject anyway, and probably on many others!), goal-setting was a good idea for other people but not for me. Now, for any of you who relate to this, let me say that I now think that's just another way of not taking responsibility for our lives. It was certainly true for me. By not making clear and specific goals in the important areas of my life I was really saying I'll let life drift on by and see what happens rather than acknowledging that it's all up to me. That way I can carry on complaining about my career and my bank balance without really having to do anything about it.

But I can also proudly hold my hand up and say I've changed all that in the last year or so – and what a difference it has made. The areas where I had been struggling – around my career (what direction to go in) and money (not enough of it!) – have altered remarkably and dramatically. All because I became clear about what I wanted and then took action. In the last year I've taken my work in a whole new direction, created and led many courses, become a tutor for the inspirational Isbourne Holistic Centre (tag line 'creating positive lives through holistic education'. www.isbourne.org), done public speaking events, appeared on live radio several times, extended my corporate work, have a full client list, tripled my income and I've written the book I've been talking about for the last three years – the one you're reading!

And this was all because I started becoming very clear about what I wanted, when I wanted it by and then taking action.

Now there has been one other key magic ingredient that I had been neglecting for years as a person running my own business. You want to know what it is, don't you? Can you too have that key magic ingredient? The answer is yes because it's…drum roll…other people. You see, as a self-employed person I had fallen into the trap of believing that I had to do it all on my own. (This trap doesn't only appear in the area of work. Lots of us think that we have to sort out many areas of our lives on our own.) It was only when I realised that the coach (me) had to get a coach (the wonderful Pam Lidford www.pamlidford.co.uk) that my career and finances started to improve. It was only when I realised that my book wasn't going to get written without support and I found the inspirational Alison Thompson (aka The Proof Fairy www.theprooffairy.com) to mentor

CHAPTER TEN – DECIDE WHAT YOU WANT AND DO IT

and cajole me that I was able to write this book. (I highly recommend Alison's book coaching skills. Her strap line 'helping you take your book from possibility to plan to publication' is undoubtedly true.)

So hopefully I've been very clear as to why it's so important to decide what you want. Now to the 'doing it' bit. Because of course deciding what you want on its own isn't enough. Even if you're crystal clear about what exactly you want, down to the last itsy bitsy detail, you still have to take action to make it happen. This is when so many of the bogey men (women?) mentioned in previous chapters can jump out and scare you. This is when your limiting beliefs, your ego, your frightened inner child and your sudden fondness for your comfort zone come out of the woodwork and say 'boo'. Obviously not if you're booking a holiday (although the cost might be a bit scary!) but if you're wanting to start your own business, move to a different part of the country (move country), leave your partner, meet a partner, go sky-diving, anything new and different and challenging, then it can feel daunting to say the least.

To deal with these lurking beasties, I'm a great fan of Nike's strap line 'Just do it'. The longer we think about doing something, the greater the opportunity for our fears to multiply, alongside our ability to procrastinate. (Procrastination, by the way, is usually because we either fear doing something or because we have a perfect image of how that thing should be in our head and don't want to disappoint ourselves with the reality.) Put another way, we can think about, contemplate, consider the options, investigate, research, analyze, be almost ready to and maybe, at a push, be just about to, but nothing, I repeat NOTHING, can take the place of just doing it.

In reality, the price we pay when we don't 'just do it' and spend our lives thinking about it instead ('just think about it' isn't such a great strap line, is it? Doesn't have quite the same zing somehow!) is far greater than if we 'just do it' and it doesn't go according to plan or we fall flat on our face. The price we pay is that we're putting our lives on hold, preventing ourselves from achieving, experiencing, having, fulfilling and many other 'ings' that would make such a difference to us.

Here's a quote I often use when working with clients on this issue:

"First you jump off the cliff and you build wings on the way down." Ray Bradbury

I think this is a beautiful way of describing taking a leap of faith. Much as we'd prefer to, we can't always know the outcome of our actions before we've taken them.

My client Anya came to me knowing she wanted to help people with her healing abilities and that was as far as she'd got. When we started to talk about this further, she confided in me that she had a dream – to start a healing centre. However, she hadn't voiced her dream before because it seemed like such a big one. As we continued working on this together, she found herself admitting that she wanted her healing centre to be in Greece – an even bigger dream. So together we began to formulate a plan, bit by bit, step by step. Eventually she

CHAPTER TEN – DECIDE WHAT YOU WANT AND DO IT

found a run-down old building in Greece that she was able to buy for a fraction of the cost of a similar building here and gradually, over a period of time, she did go on to create her healing centre. But this would never have happened if she hadn't dared to voice her dream, formulate a plan and then take action.

There are many theories about manifestation and what does and doesn't already exist in the world. Some people say that everything we want already exists at some level. The way I like to think about it is that anything and everything that has been created must have always been possible – sort of floating in the ether waiting for us to tune into it. For example, in order to build the first airplane, the potential to do it must always have existed. We just needed someone with enough vision and determination, together with the skills and abilities to make it happen.

So what if that's true for anything that you want to have, be or do? Maybe it's all possible. It just needs you to become clear about what you want (i.e. create a vision), be determined to create it (and gain the necessary skills) and then take the steps to make it happen.

There are many good books on The Law of Attraction i.e. our ability to create whatever we want in our lives, so I'm not going to go into that. 'The Secret' by Rhonda Byrne is probably one of the better known ones and makes it easy to take on board the idea. But what I will say is that from my own experience, the clearer I've become about what I've wanted in my life, the more determined I've been to make it happen, the more easily I've been able to manifest what might be called miracles – or they certainly seemed that way to me at the time.

A couple of examples:

When I did my coaching course, I initially went on an open day to find out more about it. By the end of the day I was absolutely clear that I wanted to do it. This was the right thing for me, my next step, my new brilliant career. Except I didn't have the £2,500 to do the course – not a penny of it. Now I had volunteered to be a guinea pig on the open day to do an exercise clarifying intention. When we finished the exercise, I knew with every fibre of my being that I would have that £2,500 two months later by the start of the course. And I did. I didn't beg, borrow or steal it (in fact right now I don't know how I got it). All I know is that the money was there when I needed it. So that was a really good example of a SMART goal. "I want £2,500 by January 30th 2004 to do my coaching course".

The second example is a fun one. I very much wanted to have a Mercedes SLK. I just loved those cars (and still do!). However, the car I was driving at the time was a Vauxhall Nova (remember those?) so you can tell that I didn't quite have the financial wherewithal to go and buy my SLK.

However, I created a vision board instead. This is such a fun thing to do. You start with a large piece of cardboard and then find as many images as you can (from magazines, the internet, photos) that represent things you want in your life. It might be a house, a car, a healthy lifestyle, inner peace. Just put those images together with any words or phrases that are meaningful to you (such as 'feeling full of energy' or 'my fantastic relationship') on the board. You can also add money or write a cheque to yourself for however much money you would like to attract into your life and stick that on. Then put a photo of yourself somewhere on the board (in my case I was in the driving seat of the SLK!) and add the words "for the highest good of all concerned". This is important because you don't want to acquire any of this at anyone else's expense e.g. from someone's will.

So I did all this with my SLK and a month later I met a new man. Guess what car he drove?! He was subsequently kind enough to put me on his insurance so I had a sexy SLK to drive without having to pay for petrol, insurance, repairs… The Universe had given me what I wanted in a far better way than I could have imagined, together with a fabulous man to boot! (Note to reader: I was attracted to the man first before I even knew about his car!)

So what is it that you want? And what are you going to do to get it?

Exercise:

1. Decide on one thing you'd like that would really make a difference in your life and write that down.

2. Now make it into a SMART goal. Remember, if the initial goal is too big, then break it down into a series of smaller steps.

3. Finally commit to taking your first step and be specific about what it is and when you're going to do it. No letting yourself off the hook now! A tip here. We're often very good at keeping our commitments to other people and not so great at keeping commitments to ourselves.

So choose a trusted friend and tell them what your step is and what your deadline is. Ask them to check with you on the deadline date. So you're being checked up on now. Better get going!

CHAPTER ELEVEN - LIVING RIGHT HERE, RIGHT NOW

"Yesterday is gone. Tomorrow has not yet come. We have only today. Let us begin."

Mother Teresa

You know how it is with little children. They laugh, they cry, they play, they throw a tantrum. But always they're concerned with what they're doing in the here and now. And, for the most part, don't they have fun. We were all like that once. We all had the ability to be fully involved and engrossed in our present moment. (I know my son does from the number of times he doesn't hear me when I ask him to do something. I used to think he was simply selectively tuning out – and in a way he is. But it's also because he is SO engaged with what he's doing that he actually doesn't hear me.) Then as time goes by and life takes on a more serious quality (jobs, families, bills to pay) we somehow lose that ability.

By the time we're adults most of us wander through our days unaware of how much time we spend reflecting on the past (often with guilt, regret and who knows how many other sticks to beat ourselves with) or wondering about the future (often with fear and trepidation). Now isn't this a ridiculous thing to do to ourselves? And whether we're mainly stuck in the past or jumping to the future, the one moment we're missing is NOW.

When do we spot the spider's web covered in dew, the child skipping with joy, the once-in-a-lifetime-never-to-be-repeated sunset?

The answer, of course, is only ever NOW.

We want more joy, happiness and well-being in our lives. When are we going to experience that? We can only have it now. There's no possibility of retrospective happiness. It only exists in the present moment. Let me be clear here that I'm talking about true happiness rather than looking back into the past and wishing we were there because we were happy then. All that does is shift our focus away from the present so we don't have to deal with it. It's an emotional escape route rather than a true source of happiness.

Same with living in the future. If we're hanging out there in our minds more often than being in the present (because we've got a fabulous future fantasy going on) then we're avoiding what actually exists right here, right now, including the possibility of changing anything. Or if we live in a fearful future in our heads, yanking ourselves back to the present will greatly diminish those fears. As discussed in the chapter on 'Fear', if we are able to train our minds not to wander off down frightening alleyways into the future, we would see that none of what we're imagining is happening right now (nor is it very likely to happen in the future).

If you can look at it this way, your whole life is a series of present moments. It is the only time that really exists. Everything else is in our heads.

Recently I watched a TV programme called 'Man Made Home' in

CHAPTER ELEVEN – LIVING RIGHT HERE, RIGHT NOW

which TV presenter Kevin McCloud builds a hut in a field and then transports it to the coast. The premise of the series is to discover whether happiness can be increased by taking used and unwanted items (mostly found locally) and turning them into something useful and beautiful, in this case for his hut (rather than following the current obsession with buying something new and shiny). Apart from the brilliance of the design ideas, what really struck me was how completely and fully engaged Kevin was with whatever he was doing. It was very apparent that he was experiencing such child-like joy and pleasure from his activities. He actually talked about feeling like a young boy and perhaps there's the key to eternal youth (in our minds anyway), completely immersing ourselves in whatever activity we're involved with.

Now you might say, "Well he was doing something he really enjoyed in the first place." To which I would reply, "What's so wrong with that?!" It would be great if more of us did more of what we enjoyed more of the time. But also, how often have you been doing something that you enjoyed, only to be thinking about something in the past or future? How often have I been playing with my son, only to be thinking about yesterday's client or that evening's supper?

So, if the present moment is the only time we can really experience our lives, the next challenge is to make that experience as positive as possible. "But what if something awful is going on in the present moment?" I hear you cry. In answer I would say that most of the time there's something good to be found in any moment if you choose to look for it.

Flashback fifteen years or so and I had fallen in love with an Aussie surfer. (Or so I thought at the time – the falling in love bit – he was definitely an Aussie surfer!) I'd met him in London and when he went back to Australia I followed him out (at his invitation) three times and on each occasion he ended the relationship not long after I got there. (Yes, I know, how stupid can you be? Clearly I can be very stupid but hopefully I'm not only older but also a tad wiser now.) Anyway, after the third of these 'dumping' occasions feeling as though my heart would break, I decided to go out for a run just to do something, anything, other than sit around and feel sorry for myself.

As I ran through the Australian bush on that gloriously sunny, blue-sky afternoon, I was suddenly profoundly aware that I had a choice. I could continue to run with tears streaming down my face. Or I could marvel at the stunning scenery, relish the sun on my back and experience joy that my body was feeling so alive as I ran. Thankfully I made the latter choice and suddenly went from feeling like I was falling apart to feeling fantastic. Nothing had changed in the outside world. I was still in Australia, on my own and well and truly dumped. But I had changed my focus from misery to pleasure.

Note to my readers. Talking about being 'dumped' is great victim speak. Please do not use the phrase except to send yourself up!

So whenever you're feeling less than happy, check with yourself where your thoughts are predominantly focused. If they're anywhere but in the present moment, haul them back in and start to pay attention to

CHAPTER ELEVEN – LIVING RIGHT HERE, RIGHT NOW

what's actually happening right now.

I'm practising it myself as I type this. I notice that I'm thinking about my son, who's about to run through the door, and an e-mail I sent yesterday. But once I bring myself back to now, I'm able to concentrate more fully on what I'm doing and enjoy the experience of being engaged in the present moment, of writing for you, all the more.

Exercise:

Try this for yourself. Take the moment you're in and just notice what thoughts are floating through your mind. How many of them are to do with the past and how many to do with the future?

Then sit quietly for a minute or two and concentrate on what you're experiencing in the moment. What is actually happening right here, right now? If any thoughts of past or future float by (which they're likely to) just blow them away like passing clouds.

Notice what it feels like to be fully present in the now and hold me responsible for any greater experience of inner peace or well-being!

CHAPTER TWELVE – SOME THINGS TO HELP YOU ON THE JOURNEY WITH NO DISTANCE

"Faith is taking the first step even when you can't see the whole staircase."

Martin Luther King

I couldn't complete this book without delving deep into my Mary Poppins carpet bag of thoughts and ideas to share with you. If you've never watched Mary Poppins, first of all 'do' and secondly, her carpet bag contained all sorts of wondrous things, far too many to fit into the bag from which they came. Actually, as I write this, what a great metaphor for our lives. Perhaps there is far, far more to all of us than we can imagine or believe is possible. "Wow, is all of that me?" I would like to hear you say. "Can I really be that amazing? Are all these gifts, talents and abilities really contained in the one 'me'?" To which I would answer: "Undoubtedly yes!"

Anyway, back to the thoughts and ideas at the bottom of my (never-empty) magic bag.

In this last chapter (yes, I know. It's sad, isn't it!) I'd like to talk a little bit about Faith, Joy and Gratitude, three Good Fairies waiting to wave their magic wands over you if you'll only just let them.

I know, truly I do, that it's all too easy to become dispirited in this world. There's much 'out there' that we can feel gloomy about if we choose. There's much in our own minds that we can allow to distract

CHAPTER TWELVE – THINGS TO HELP YOU ON THE JOURNEY WITH NO DISTANCE

us from the truth of who we are. However, as well as everything I've already talked about, I believe that focusing our lives on faith, joy and gratitude can make an immense difference. And, as with everything else in this book, they're already there if you care to look in their direction. (Look, there they are, waving madly at you right now!)

Let's start with the first good fairy – Faith. Faith can mean many different things to different people. You might understand the word to mean faith in God, in a higher power, in the Universe, in yourself… Whatever your definition, I think having faith is always about believing in something that is beyond logic, inexplicable to and unreachable by the rational mind (in fact the rational mind can be seen as the enemy of faith). Faith is about knowing with an inner wisdom, trusting with your heart, that things will work out for you in the end (even if they don't seem to be right now). Faith is about believing that the world (God, the Universe) is essentially wanting to support you in being whole, healthy and happy.

In the words of Albert Einstein, "The most important decision we make is whether we live in a friendly or hostile world".

What would your life be like if you could cultivate an unshakeable faith that the world was your friend, that it wanted to give you a good life and possibly the only thing standing in the way is – you! The phrase 'I'm my own worst enemy' takes on a whole new meaning. What you believe about yourself, you'll tend to believe about the world as a whole. So if you lack faith in yourself then it figures that you'll find it difficult to have faith in the world. Conversely if you have faith in yourself, your abilities, your qualities, your innate value as a human being then it's more likely that you can have faith in the world you live in.

What would it be like to wake up every day and have faith that today the world is conspiring to bring you all things good? That may not end up being the ultimate reality of your day but I can pretty much guarantee that you'll have a heck of a better day than if you begin it without that faith and belief.

Faith, to me, is a bridge between current and future reality. If you want to move from where you are currently (in any aspect of your life) to where you want to be then it really helps to have faith that you can make the leap. Faith in yourself and, if you choose, faith in something greater than you.

Faith is also a pathway to the Big G (please insert the God of your choice if you have one). Let me tell you a story about me and God. As I've mentioned, I discovered that I wanted God to be a part of my life during an exercise in a seminar. From that moment on I knew somewhere in the very fibre of my being that God was real. But what was God? How could I prove to myself that He existed? How could I reconcile knowing He existed but not being able to talk with conviction about why I knew that? (No, I know I wasn't alone with this challenge!)

I spent years pondering, deliberating, searching until I finally understood that my answer was never going to be found through thinking about it. I had to let go of reason and logic and embrace faith. Suddenly when I could genuinely say "I have faith that God exists" I had found my answer. Not because I'd copped out and got fed up with asking the questions but because I'd finally accessed another part of my being: a deeper, wiser, more knowing part.

So perhaps it's the same with anything we want in life – whether it's God or the man/woman of our dreams. If we have faith that he/she exists, we are so much more likely to find them.

Faith keeps you moving forward when you might otherwise have given up. Faith motivates and inspires you. Faith is like a torch bearer at the front of the parade saying "Walk this way. I'll light your path and show you where to go." I recommend it highly!

Now on to the second good fairy – Joy. I think in a way there are two types of joy. This might sound a little strange but bear with me.

The first type is the experience of joy. When was the last time you experienced any joy in your life? I may be being presumptuous here but do you even remember what it feels like to be joyful? I ask these questions not because you are a miserable slug of the universe but because these days most of us lead such busy, crazy, hectic lives that we don't take the time to allow the experience of joy.

Joy is something that takes a moment of awareness, of being in the present, to acknowledge something or someone that makes you joyful. There is so much around us every day that has the potential to bring joy and yet we're in too much of a hurry to get to the next moment and so we miss the one containing the joy.

I was working with a client recently who was talking about wanting to relax more in life so we started looking at things she found relaxing. Walking the dog round a local lake came high on the list. When I asked if she stopped to enjoy anything on the way, she suddenly looked tearful. "Oh my goodness, the ducks!" was her reply. I asked her why she was tearful and she told me that she loved ducks but never spent a single moment stopping to enjoy and find joy in them. She walked the dog the same way she did everything else – going nineteen to the dozen with the aim of getting round the lake as quickly as possible so she could then unload the dishwasher etc. Where's the joy in that?

I also think there's a deeper form of joy, one that isn't dependent on an experience or situation. This is the innate joy that's present within us always. It's part of the very fabric of our being. This joy is part of who we are if we'd only allow ourselves to feel its existence. All too often our joy is overshadowed by our busyness, our past or future thoughts and numerous clouds that flit across our minds, masking its presence. It's so easy to see this joy in small children but by the time we become adult, we've forgotten (by and large) how to allow ourselves to be joyful.

When I'd finished my first personal development seminar, having peeled away so many layers of my defenses, I left there feeling more open and loving than I had in a long time. I remember walking through Marks & Spencer (the spiritual home of The Shopper) afterwards feeling so joyful and recognising that I was experiencing

CHAPTER TWELVE – THINGS TO HELP YOU ON THE JOURNEY WITH NO DISTANCE

my true self before time had re-shaped my thoughts about myself and life. This joy wasn't about anything in particular. It was about being me (and a natural bonus of being in this state was to feel so loving towards everyone in the shop. I could have walked round M&S hugging everyone but restrained myself!). I knew the feeling of joy wouldn't (couldn't) last forever but it was wonderful while it was there and served as a huge reminder that we all have access to that joy if we choose. I wasn't a different person from the one who had gone into the seminar; I was simply more fully and truly me. And it was inevitable that I would be joyful as part of my (and everyone else's) natural state of being.

So I'd like my story to serve as a reminder that we all have that innate, indestructible, indescribably delicious joy curled up somewhere in the depths of our being. It's waiting for a nod and a wave from us to allow it to come out to play.

And finally the third good fairy, Gratitude. I personally don't know of anything more powerful to shift our perception of ourselves and our world from negative to positive in an instant than gratitude.

It is all too easy in today's world to be aware of what we don't have rather than appreciating and valuing what we do have. We live in such a 'have more, be more, do more' culture and whilst it's great to aspire, it's lousy to feel lack (whether that's inner or outer).

If you were to take a moment and think about all the things you're truly grateful for in your life, you'd be amazed at how long this list becomes. Yes, you might start off feeling grouchy and thinking,

"There isn't much to be grateful for right now." But if you open your heart and allow yourself to acknowledge the people who add to your life in some way, all the love, support and encouragement you've received (past and present), isn't that something to be grateful for? If you then add all the great experiences you've had, all you've learnt, all you currently have in your life, you could find yourself with a very long list.

Ultimately gratitude, as with everything else in this book, is about awareness and choice. How do you want to feel about yourself and the world around you? Do you want to spend your days feeling resentful and inwardly shrivelled through focusing on everything that's wrong and all that you don't have? Or would you prefer to live with a daily appreciation of all the goodness, gifts and gorgeousness that's around you if you choose to see it? When put like that, surely there is only one choice.

I notice, as I write this, that I have a huge feeling of gratitude swelling in my heart. It's not even about anything specific but a deep inner knowledge that I do have so much to be grateful for. As I focus on this feeling, I notice that all is well with the world and all is well with me.

One final story. I went on a week-long yoga retreat for my 50th birthday (a fabulous gift from me to me!) It was with a gorgeous and inspirational woman called Maya Fiennes (www.mayaspace.com). On the last morning of the retreat, we'd finished our morning mantras and I suddenly found myself crying and crying……and crying some more. I cried more than I can ever remember. I cried bucket loads

CHAPTER TWELVE – THINGS TO HELP YOU ON THE JOURNEY WITH NO DISTANCE

(definite wet patch on the carpet around me). But those tears were tears of total and utter gratitude. In those moments I was more aware at a deep and profound level of just how much I had to be grateful for. I felt gratitude for all that I am, all that I have and all that is good in the world. I also knew (perhaps this was on reflection afterwards) that this gratitude is there within me always. I just need to remember that. The me I had taken into the yoga retreat was no different from the me who left it simply glowing with gratitude. Yes, I had chanted and contorted and Maya had been fantastic. But ultimately and essentially that gratitude was already there. It was, and is, there in me. It's there in you too. And I feel very grateful for that.

There is no exercise at the end of this chapter, only a request for you to have faith in yourself and the world around you; to have joy in your life and be joyful and for you to be deeply grateful for all that you are and all that you have. Faith, Joy and Gratitude – let them sprinkle their fairy dust over you and may your days be full of magic.

CONCLUSION

"You had the power all along, my dear."
Glinda the Good Witch from The Wizard of Oz

So how was it for you? My deepest wish is that you finish this book feeling that you've learnt something about yourself, that you have a clearer map of how to be happy, that you've put some more pieces of your inner jigsaw puzzle together. More than anything, I want you to know that you are everything you need and you have everything you need to create everything you want.

I hope your inner bell has rung a few times as you recognised that what I've said is true for you (and for us all). I hope you've laughed a little. And I hope you finish this book feeling happier, more optimistic and positive about yourself and your life than when you started.

As the title says: you don't need to go anywhere or be anyone different to have a life you love.

Now put this book down, go out into the world and be the glorious, magnificent, unique you that you were put on this planet to be. Go!

ABOUT THE AUTHOR

With a background in counselling and coaching, Carrie Rose has helped hundreds of people create happier, more fulfilling and rewarding lives – both personally and professionally.

In her work with businesses, she coaches individuals and runs courses to help employees bring more of their talents and gifts to the workplace.

A popular public speaker, Carrie is dedicated to spreading the message that we all have so much potential and how to go about fulfilling it.

Carrie has had a full and varied career ranging from being a TV scriptwriter to running her own interior design business. However, it is only since working with people to help them truly flourish that she has found her life purpose.

When not inspiring others, Carrie finds her own inspiration from long walks, short swims, the Cornish Coast and being creative with her son.

Carrie is married and lives in the Cotswolds with her husband, son, stepson and brother. Yes, that is a lot of men to live with!

For further information about Carrie's work – one-to-one consultations, courses, public speaking and more – visit

www.onelifeyourlifeloveit.com

or e-mail carrie@onelifeyourlifeloveit.com

RECOMMENDED READING LIST

I have read so many helpful and inspirational books over the years that it's hard to know where to begin. But I would like to at least recommend to you some of the books that have been the most valuable to me in the hope that they will be useful to you too.

A Return to Love Marianne Williamson

Age of Miracles Marianne Williamson

Be A Free Range Human Marianne Cantwell

Callings Gregg Levoy

Embracing Your Inner Critic Hal Stone & Sidra Stone

Emotional Intelligence Daniel Goleman

Everything I've Ever Done That Worked Lesley Garner

Fearless Living Rhonda Britten

Feel the Fear and Do It Anyway Susan Jeffers

Life Strategies Dr Phillip C McGraw

Living, Loving & Healing Bernie Siegel

Living in the Light Shakti Gawain

Love is Letting Go of Fear Gerald Jampolsky

Loving What Is Byron Katie

Money Heart & Mind William Bloom

CHAPTER TWELVE – THINGS TO HELP YOU ON THE JOURNEY WITH NO DISTANCE

Notes From a Friend Anthony Robbins

Powerful Beyond Measure Nick Williams

Resisting Your Soul Nick Williams

Shift Happens Robert Holden

Speak So Your Audience Will Listen Robin Kermode

Successful but Something Missing Ben Renshaw

Success Intelligence Robert Holden

Taming Your Gremlin Rick Carson

The Business You Were Born to Create Nick Williams

The Good Marriage Helen Garlick & Jane Stuart Sheppard

The Power Is Within Louise Hay

The Power of Now Eckhart Tolle

The Power of Silence Carlos Castaneda

The Secret Rhonda Byrne

The Seven Spiritual Laws of Success Deepak Chopra

The Success Principles Jack Canfield

The Thief Who Pretended To Be a Policeman Leo Hawkins

The Work We Were Born to Do Nick Williams

Unconditional Success Nick Williams

Who Moved My Cheese? Dr Spencer Johnson

You Can Heal Your Life Louise Hay

Made in the USA
Charleston, SC
07 June 2014